How To
Choose Your
First Powerboat

How To Choose Your First Powerboat

Chuck Gould

Illustrated by Larry Dubia

SHERIDAN HOUSE

First published 1999 by
Sheridan House Inc.
145 Palisade Street
Dobbs Ferry, NY 10522

While all reasonable care has been taken in the publication of
this book, the publisher takes no responsibility for the use of the
methods or products described in the book.

Library of Congress Cataloging-in-Publication Data

Gould, Chuck
    How to choose your first powerboat / Chuck Gould; illustrated by
    Larry Dubia.
        p. cm.
    ISBN 1-57409-056-9 (alk. paper)
    1. Motorboats—Purchasing. I. Title.
VM341.G643 1999
623.8'231'0297—dc21   98-47033
                                                              CIP

Illustrations by Larry Dubia

Printed in the United States of America

ISBN 1-57049-056-9

CONTENTS

PART II   INSPECTING THE PRIMARY SYSTEMS

PART III   EVALUATING THE SECONDARY SYSTEMS

PART IV   LET'S MAKE A DEAL

PART ONE

General Considerations

1

Welcome Aboard!

IF YOU ARE CONSIDERING the purchase of your first powerboat, congratulations! With the possible exception of a home, most of us will never make a purchase that requires a larger financial commitment or can make such a positive difference in our lifestyles. As a boater, you will quickly discover that some of the nicest people just happen to spend their spare time on the water. Many boaters shopping for their second boat are doing so much sooner than they ever anticipated, and can be heard to exclaim, "Gee, I sure wish we'd known about that *before* we bought a boat!"

This book enables the first-time boat buyer to select a boat without risking the potentially catastrophic expense of purchasing (and having to quickly resell) an unsuitable boat. New boaters have been known to drop out of boating entirely because of disappointment with their choice of a boat. Considering that boating is one of the most incredible ways to occupy leisure time, missing out as the result of an underinformed decision would certainly be a shame.

THE FINE ART OF COMPROMISE

By its very nature, any boat is a floating compromise. Even with an unlimited budget, a blank draftsman's sheet, and a degree in naval architecture, most experienced boaters

3

would still be unable to design a single craft to fulfill all their needs and desires. Some characteristics a boater might desire, such as "able to cruise easily at 15 knots" or "easily docked by two people," will always conflict with other possible priorities such as "exceptional fuel economy" or "space for a grand piano in the saloon." Combining the priorities of a second party, such as a spouse, will create the need for even more compromises and evaluations. Just as there is no perfect home, car, occupation, or haircut that will be best for everyone, there is no secret boat so clearly superior in concept and execution that every wise and experienced boater would always choose above any other option.

ONE DEFINITION OF SUCCESS

The most successful boat purchases are those that reflect the right combination of compromises, and that, by virtue of appropriate design, initial construction, and present condition, allow the maximum boating experience by the owners, their family, or guests.

2

Introspection Precedes Boat Inspection

THE FRIENDS AND FAMILY FACTOR

Boats have, without a doubt, been successfully purchased by people who gave more thought to the color of the upholstery than to the actual manner in which they anticipated cruising. Fortunes have also been won in Las Vegas on a single roll of the dice, but Dad's advice was right: "Don't count on it." Some self- and family evaluation will play an essential role in selecting a vessel that will be a proper fit.

Children, Teenagers, and Adults

How many people will customarily cruise with you, and how many are children? Kids on a boat present special joys and challenges. Any nonswimmers and especially the very young benefit from features such as adequate side decks and sturdy railings, as well as enough wiggle room aboard to allow for the wearing of personal flotation devices while underway. With kids, space for some type of activity aboard, whether reading, playing cards, watching a video, or coloring with crayons, can be important. Most children are fascinated with "just being on a boat" for about the first two hours but require some diversion thereafter. Teenagers (prepare to be shocked) appreciate adequate shower and grooming facilities and will guard whatever shred of privacy they can establish on a boat just as jealously as at home. Kids of all ages will often ask to bring a friend along on a weekend outing, and some of your landlocked adult friends may express an increased interest in spending time with you as well (just to prevent you from becoming too "lonely" on your new boat, you understand). So it might be well to plan for a cruising crowd of up to twice the size of your family on occasion. In general, boaters are a social crowd, and unless you intend to lock yourself on board and draw the curtains when visiting a marina, there's a real probability that you will meet more new friends and genuinely interesting acquaintances when boating than in any other activity. *Be prepared to entertain.*

EFFECTS OF FRIENDS AND FAMILY ON DESIGN

Younger kids may tolerate sleeping arrangements created by dropping the galley table and covering it with cushions, or pulling out a sofa sleeper in the saloon. But should you be likely to cruise frequently with other adults, at least one semi-private area per couple is a preferred arrangement. Beginning with boats in the low to mid 30-foot range, second heads are commonly available and should be given consideration when cruising with adults or teenagers.

Getting on and off some boats can be difficult for the very young or for the most senior family members. A boat design that requires everyone to scale a ladder up a tall transom may allow for a larger aft stateroom and additional deck space, but might not be the best choice for a family with members who are less than able or comfortable in climbing. One of those compromises, again.

The Concept of Self-Containment

A boat is a self-contained environment. The greater the number of people aboard and the longer the anticipated cruise, the more capacity will be needed to store freshwater, food and fuel, and to contain waste. Cruising with six people for a week on a boat with a 50-gallon freshwater tank and a 20-gallon holding tank could put you at the dock for purposes of refilling the freshwater and using the pump-out more often than you might prefer.

Additional Recreational Activities

What other activities will you pursue when boating? Fishing, diving, entertaining large groups, sunbathing, etc. may all require boats with design elements emphasizing different allocations and priorities of deck layout and design.

Seasonal Considerations

When will you use the boat? If you will be doing your boating primarily on two-day weekends and your intended cruising grounds are any great distance from your permanent moorage, it may be well to consider a vessel with a greater speed potential. If you plan to use your boat year-round, adequate cabin heat both dockside and underway is a must in northern climates, as well as a sturdy hull with freeboard adequate to ride out moderate storms. Winter boaters appreciate boats with an inside helm station. Boat builders with large warm weather markets often supply boats with helms on the fly bridge only, and consider an inside helm station to be optional. In addition to allowing operation of the boat from a warm and dry environment, the inside helm increases safety by establishing a second set of controls for engine, transmission, and steering in the event of the failure of either set of controls (a rare, but possible situation).

CONSIDER THE CRUISING ENVIRONMENT

Under what conditions will you be boating? For safety considerations a boat should be capable of withstanding the roughest conditions to which it will ever be subjected, rather than be merely suitable for its "normal" usage. Boaters who venture once a year from sheltered inland waters out into the open ocean in search of salmon, tuna, or sailfish are wise to select a vessel that is suitable for the open ocean, even though they might be considered over-equipped (an oxymoron on a boat) for customary inland cruising.

Tides and Currents

If a boat will ever be operated in areas known for strong currents, such as in a river or narrow inter-island passages in strong tidal areas, adequate power will be required. Unless a boater heads downstream or can wait for either a slack or favorable tide, the speed of the opposing current must be deducted from the normal cruising speed of the boat when calculating actual velocity made good. A boat with a top speed of seven knots running against a 6-knot current would need all afternoon to get out of sight of the dock.

TIME AND MONEY ISSUES

How much time will you enjoy devoting to noncruising activities such as cleaning and repair? The gleaming, classic, mahogany-hulled cruiser that turns heads and garners compliments in every marina is in that condition due to the probable expenditure of one or two hours cleaning, sanding, or varnishing for every hour spent underway. If acquired by a skipper with a tendency to procrastinate on maintenance, the same vessel will cause the same turned heads to shake in a chorus of "isn't it a shame." Generally the older the boat, the more wood will be found on the exterior. Whether sanded and painted or sanded and coated with 8 to 10 hand-laid coats of varnish, nothing looks better when it's well cared for (or worse, when neglected) than wood on a boat. Fiberglass requires cleaning and waxing as well to protect the gelcoat finish and to maintain the appearance of the boat.

New or Used?

Once the inevitable bugs have been worked out, purchasers of new boats can expect at least a brief period when nearly every system on the boat is working correctly almost all of the time. Buyers of older boats can expect to plow some of the savings realized by purchasing a partially depreciated vessel back into the boat, as many of the bugs worked out of the boat when new have worked their way back again and brought along some relatives as well. The first economic rule of recreational boating states, "Money not spent to get afloat will be spent to stay afloat." And so it shall.

ALLOCATION OF SPACE

Space on most cruising powerboats can be divided into the following areas. The exterior will typically consist of a foredeck, port and starboard side decks, the aft deck or cockpit, and the flying bridge. Interior spaces will usually feature a main saloon, a master stateroom, one or more heads, and a galley. Additional guest staterooms increase in number as a boat increases in length and beam, and other areas become larger and more lavishly equipped on larger vessels. The engine room and the anchor locker are important areas below decks as well. Without multi-story superstructures there is a difficulty in maximizing both interior and exterior spaces on a boat. Too much superstructure, however, may create a craft that is either top heavy or provides too large an area for unfavorable winds to impact. Imagine trying to dock a billboard in a cross wind.

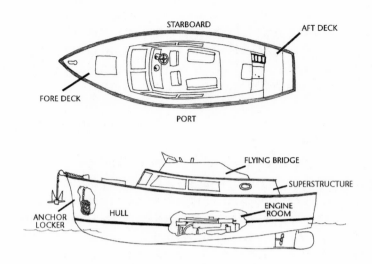

Space divisions common to powerboats.

Some contemplation of the who, what, where, and when questions will assist the novice boat buyer in imagining a general allocation of spaces itemized in the previous paragraph. For example, sunworshipers (who may possibly be entertaining onlooking boaters by baking themselves to a tan) will prefer more deck space, while a gourmet chef who will be entertaining visitors by baking a soufflé for eight will allocate a greater amount of space to the galley and the main saloon.

For most people the perfect boat does not exist, but identifying the relationship between the allocation of space and the boater's own cruising agenda will be of great benefit when considering the wide variety of boat designs available.

3

How Large a Boat?

COST VS. FUN

For many people, the answer to the question of how large a boat to buy is automatically "the largest one we can afford!" There is an often painfully obvious relationship between a boat's size and the exponentially increasing cost of owning one. In the fantasies of most boaters, we see ourselves lounging with a bottle of the finest champagne on the deck of our immaculately maintained 120-foot ocean-traversing yacht, anchored in an exotic tropical harbor, where warm tropical breezes waft slowly across the water. While for a fortunate few this may represent reality, the majority of us powerboaters seem to be opening a can of beer on a 25- to 42-foot boat, at the public dock, while hoping it doesn't rain again this weekend. Luckily, for most boaters it is possible to enjoy boating in a humble runabout with a canvas top almost as much as in a megamillion-dollar luxury liner. In fact some who could experience both might actually prefer the closer-to-nature experience of the smaller boat.

CHALLENGES OF A LARGE BOAT

Factors other than cost and affordability should enter into a full consideration of size. Larger boats require more expensive monthly moorage. Slips longer than 40 feet are often hard to find, making it difficult to change the boat's location, and the marina manager may feel no great urgency to price a rarely available slip in a competitive manner. Larger boats will consume more time and/or money for cleaning and maintenance tasks. Too large a vessel may tax the docking and maneuvering skills of a new boater or the physical capabilities of a post-retirement couple to a potentially disastrous degree. At any marina it is possible to observe boats of 60 feet or larger being successfully and adeptly docked by a cruising couple, but it is unfortunately also common to see boats of 36 feet or less pinballing around and clearly beyond the boat-handling skills of skipper and crew. When perusing broker or private-party ads for larger boats it is not unusual in the least to see a comment, "Willing to accept smaller boat as partial payment."

PROBLEMS OF A SMALL BOAT

A boat needs to be large enough to safely handle the worst weather which it will ever encounter. The smaller the boat, the more optimistic the weather forecast must be before deciding to leave the dock or launch from the trailer. While no boat is large enough to intelligently begin cruising under gale or storm conditions, sometimes the weather can change more quickly than expected, and those out in the smaller boats suffer the worst. If you have a small boat, better carry a big barometer (and keep mental track of the closest available shelter at all times). Smaller boats present special challenges in stowage of gear and supplies. The recent purchaser of a new boat was heard to complain that "by the time we got all of the Coast Guard-required equipment aboard, there was no room for groceries!"

Purchasing a much smaller boat than required is no more advisable than moving the entire family into a one-bedroom cabin.

A STARTER BOAT?

Buying too small a boat will put a boater back into the market very quickly, with all of the hassle and expense of trading in or selling the small boat. It can be a mistake to conclude that stepping up to the next size of boat will necessarily be as easy or inexpensive as trading up to a larger Chevy, or from a Honda to a Lexus. Used boats can stay on the market for a matter of hours or as long as several years. Purchasing a much smaller boat than required as a starter boat ("to see if we like boating") is no more advisable than moving the entire family into a one-bedroom cabin to try out home ownership. Cramming everybody and everything into a tiny space on a hull of inadequate seaworthiness is more likely to result in the entire family developing a quick and enduring disdain for boating than to spark a life-long love affair with spending time at sea. Chartering a boat is an excellent way to give boating a trial before buying a boat, and is much less expensive than buying a vessel acknowledged to be inadequate from the beginning.

EFFECTS OF BOAT DESIGN ON LENGTH

By taking a thorough look at the answers to the previously considered who, when, what, how questions and examining a few boats on the market in various styles, a boat buyer will begin to formulate an opinion on a range of suitable sizes. Size requirements will vary between design concepts. A boater seeking two large staterooms might be fairly content with a 34- to 36-foot tricabin design. But if the same boater desires a roomy cockpit for fishing, he or she might need to consider a 42-foot sportfisherman to achieve the same amount of usable interior space.

Effect of Beam on Size

A longer boat isn't always a larger boat. The beam (width) of a boat will have a significant influence on the overall size of the craft. While boats are not rectangular in shape, a relatively rough size comparison can still be achieved by multiplying the length of the hull by the beam. For example, a 34-foot boat with a 10-foot beam (34 x 10 = 340) would not really be larger than a 32-foot boat with an 11-foot beam (32 x 11 = 352). A 36-foot boat with a 12-foot beam would factor out to 432, while a 40-foot boat with a 14-foot beam would multiply to 560—a case where a boat only 11 percent longer is actually about one-third bigger. Boat builders have been offering vessels with more beam in recent years, leaving some 20- and 30-year-old boats looking almost skinny by comparison.

Confusing Manufacturer Claims

Boats can be measured by different standards. One manufacturer may build a hull 28-foot long down the center, hang a two-foot swim step off the stern, add two feet of pulpit to the bow and market the boat as a 32 footer. Another manu-

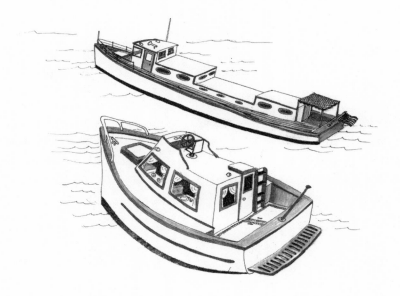

A longer boat isn't always a larger boat.

facturer may label a boat as a "Pileknocker 44" but actually deliver a craft that will take every bit of 50 feet of dock space when pulpits and swim steps are accounted for. (Owners of such vessels often emphasize the 50-foot length when describing the boat to friends and the 44-foot designation when paying per foot for an evening at a marina.)

To a casual observer the non-standardization of boat measurement is reminiscent of the story of the traveling rug merchant. When a customer entered the rug merchant's tent, the merchant called out to his assistant to bring the measuring stick. The assistant was heard to reply, "Which stick, master? The one for buying or the one for selling?" When comparing boats it is well to understand whether the measurement being used is the LWL (length of water line), LOA (length overall), or some other measurement entirely.

4

Common Powerboat Varieties

MANUFACTURERS USE DIFFERENT terminology to identify the boats in their product lines. Some consistent definitions have emerged for various configurations and hull designs, but the use of these terms is not completely universal and endless hair-splitting arguments could (and do) take place regarding the appropriate categorization for individual boats.

RUNABOUTS

The smallest practical powerboats, with the exception of motorized dinghies, are in the category known as runabouts. These boats are primarily in the 16–24 feet range and are very open, with planing hulls and designs emphasizing the achievement of high speeds under reasonably calm conditions. Runabouts are often powered by outboard motors, but

Note: The prices quoted in this chapter are taken from the *1997 ABOS Marine Blue Book,* a reference work available in most public libraries. The boats listed all have various levels of standard equipment, making true price comparison a more complicated exercise than the simple listing of numbers. The presence or absence of any make or model of boat in the "examples" section should not be construed as an endorsement or lack of same by the author.

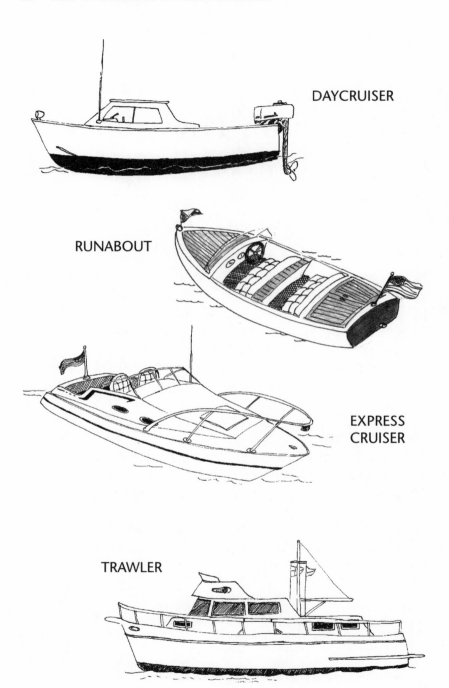

DAYCRUISER

RUNABOUT

EXPRESS
CRUISER

TRAWLER

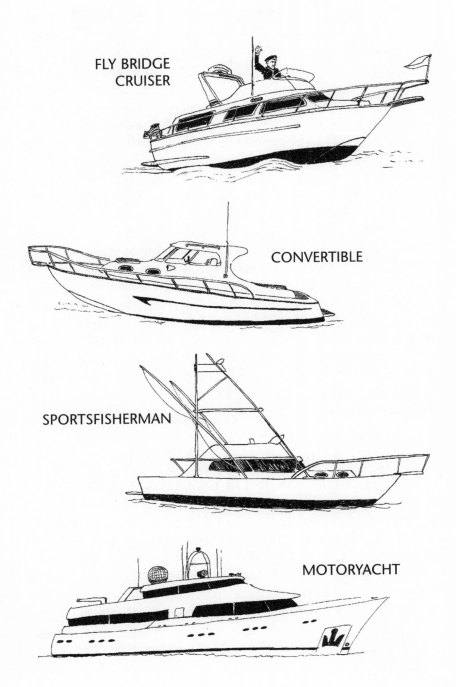

FLY BRIDGE
CRUISER

CONVERTIBLE

SPORTSFISHERMAN

MOTORYACHT

the larger sizes are frequently inboard/outboard configurations. Many runabouts maximize seating capacity with an open-bow design in which the foredeck has been replaced with installed seating. With no cooking, sleeping, or toilet provisions aboard, most runabouts are suitable for short duration only and are commonly selected for general sightseeing, waterskiing, or short-term, near-shore fishing trips. It is far more common to transport a runabout to the boating destination on a trailer and launch it at a nearby ramp than to attempt to cruise any great distance in such a vessel.

Common runabout examples—Three well known manufacturers of runabouts include Bayliner, Sea Ray, and Four Winns. There are several other major runabout builders, some of whom build very good boats. The *1997 ABOS Marine Blue Book* lists the following suggested retail prices for new runabouts: Bayliner 1851 Capri at $14,095, Sea Ray 175 Bowrider at $13,923; and Four Winns 170 Horizon at $14,903. Bayliner and Sea Ray are both divisions of the Brunswick Corporation, and Bayliner is the largest-selling brand name in powerboating. As with any product, there are many opinions regarding the integrity and intrinsic quality (or lack thereof) of any boat builder in the mass production business.

DAY CRUISERS OR CUDDY CABINS

Beginning with boats around 19 feet or so, many manufacturers provide a small, enclosed area ahead of the helm and under a raised foredeck known as a cuddy cabin. The naval architect may even have engineered a method of squeezing a small alcohol stove, a porta-potti, and a bunk or two into this area. Cuddy cabins allow boaters to seek shelter from the midday sun or a sudden rainstorm, and provide enough privacy that changing into or out of a swimsuit in a crowded

area doesn't have to become an exercise in advanced con-
tortionism and creative towel holding. Some cuddy cabins
share the same hull designs that their respective manufacturers use for their runabout line. The rudimentary cooking
and sanitation facilities allow more extended use than is
practicable with a runabout, but the boats are often called
day cruisers as they are ordinarily too sparsely appointed
for overnighting. Most day cruisers are less than 24 feet,
and it is common to store and transport them on trailers.

Common day cruiser examples—Bayliner has a
2052 Capri model listed in the *1997 ABOS Marine Blue Book*
at $15,895, and Sea Ray is shown with a 215 Express at
$28,692. Some marketers like to crowd the category, and
Sea Ray's designation of their 22-foot cuddy cabin boat as
an "Express Cruiser" is an excellent example of this.
Express Cruiser is a term more commonly applied to a
larger family of boats, discussed immediately following.
Remember that if the Bow Spring Boatworks introduces a
26-foot boat and calls it the "Bow Spring Trans-Oceanic
Liner," merely naming the model as such doesn't suddenly
make it magically correct for the implied purpose. The 215
Express Cruiser may indeed be an excellent boat, and it has
a fairly generous amount of cuddy cabin, but it is certainly
ambitiously named.

EXPRESS CRUISERS

In most product lines, somewhere in the 25-foot category,
day cruisers disappear and their big sisters, the express
cruisers, appear. The smallest express cruisers are among
the largest boats typically associated with trailer boating.
Express cruisers ordinarily incorporate an open cockpit at
the stern, but this cockpit area is proportionately smaller
than on a day cruiser, and far more of the boat is devoted to

enclosed cabin accommodations. The helmsman is seated on deck in an express cruiser design, and the entire main deck may be somewhat raised in order to facilitate engine room and cabin architecture. A frequent addition on an express cruiser is a removable canvas or permanent fiberglass hardtop to protect the skipper from the elements and allow the living space to expand and include the aft deck. Most utilize planing hulls and top speed is a major consideration for many express cruiser buyers. Inboard/outboard drive systems are common on express cruisers.

Express cruisers typically have adequate bunk, galley, and sanitation facilities to allow a cruising couple or small family to spend several days aboard the boat.

Express cruiser examples—One of the names associated with popular express cruisers is Carver, and they offer a 310 Express at $92,440 (again, according to the *ABOS* book). Four Winns markets a 258 Vista at $42,017; Bayliner, a 2859 Express Cruiser at $57,000; and Sea Ray, a 300 Sundancer at about $138,000.

FLY BRIDGE CRUISERS

At about 30 feet and above, the number of express cruisers offered begins falling off and the next largest boat type, the fly bridge cruiser, becomes more commonly available. Fly bridge cruisers feature a much higher upper deck than express cruisers, and allow more spacious cabin accommodations with greater provision for cabin headroom and larger windows providing a better view outside the boat. The helm is moved farther forward to the front of the fly bridge, and this position affords the helmsman maximum visibility. Semi-displacement hulls and twin engines are common in this category, and designers often place a great emphasis on achieving a decent turn of speed. Fly bridge cruisers are usually powered by inboard, fixed-prop engines as their taller design allows the engines to be installed under the cabin sole.

The majority of fly bridge cruisers have an open cockpit aft, but a significant number are built as aft cabins, where the cockpit has been eliminated and a raised deck used to create space for (typically) an elaborate master stateroom. The cockpit designs are easier to fish from and provide easier access to and from a dock or a dinghy, but nobody will dispute that the aft cabin configuration dramatically increases the usable interior space.

Fly bridge cruiser examples—The *1997 ABOS Marine Blue Book* lists a Bayliner 3788 Command Bridge at $165,000, a Mainship 34 Motor Yacht (another example of crowding the category) at $159,000, and a Carver 370 Aft Cabin at $190,000. A great many builders offer fly bridge cruisers, and, as with the examples listed above, a buyer will find that some prove to be more suitable than others.

SPORTSFISHERMEN AND CONVERTIBLES

For many boaters, one of the primary motivations for owning a boat is the thrill of pursuing large game fish in the open ocean. The boats that serve well for this purpose have large open cockpits, often with specialized "fighting chairs," and plenty of room for rigging lines and hauling gaffed fish aboard. When equipped primarily as a fishing platform (with outriggers, tuna towers, built-in bait tanks, etc.), such boats are commonly called sportsfishermen. Trophy angling is often a high-dollar activity, and many of the sportsfishermen have evolved into a dual-purpose category of boat referred to as a Convertible. Convertibles incorporate both a functional fishing cockpit and yachtlike interior accommodations and amenities in the cabin. Some of the costliest boats in the under-50-foot size are convertibles.

Sportsfishermen and convertibles ordinarily feature high output twin engines and semi-displacement hulls, allowing a quick run to fishing grounds 20 or 30 miles offshore. A flying bridge is a universal characteristic of convertibles and sportsfishermen. Seaworthiness is important in this classification. A boat caught in a sudden storm a considerable distance from the nearest harbor needs to be thoroughly equipped and well designed to withstand the punishment that a boat used strictly in inland waterways rarely encounters.

Well-known sportfisherman examples—Many manufacturers of convertibles and sportsfishermen have earned popular reputations for high quality and excellent craftsmanship. Egg Harbor, a perennial favorite, offers a 34-foot Golden Egg for as little as $211,000 ('95 price, according to the '97 *ABOS* book) and a 42-foot Golden Egg for $433,000. Hatteras, also considered a blue-ribbon builder, offers a 39-foot Convertible for $376,000 and a 46-foot version for $749,000. Bertram competes in this market with a 46-foot Convertible at $718,000, and a 54-foot model that lists at over $1 million. Lest you conclude that the entire group of sports-fishermen and convertibles is out of the question for all but the wealthy, the *ABOS* book lists a 32-foot Convertible by Luhrs with a suggested retail price of just $134,600; certainly not an exorbitant price for a boat of that size.

TRAWLERS

Trawlers incorporate displacement or semi-displacement hulls with high, flaring bows patterned after the sturdy commercial fishing boats from which the category derives its name. Trawlers are virtually 100 percent diesel powered, many of them use a single engine, and their designs traditionally emphasize fuel economy and range rather than speed. Due to their rugged design and the potential in some cases to travel several thousand miles on a single load of fuel, larger trawlers have long been a favorite of transoceanic voyagers. The greater number of trawlers have a flying bridge, but some are designated as pilot house models and feature a well-appointed interior helm station only.

Trawlers are a popular choice among boaters with previous sailing experience who (for whatever reason) have decided to take up powerboating.

The majority of trawlers are 32-foot and longer, with much of the group clustered between the 36-foot and 45-foot ranges. Trawlers provide opportunity for spacious cabin interiors with two basic designs: the tricabin which features a V-berth forward, a saloon and galley amidships, and an owner's stateroom aft, and the sedan (with an elaborate owner's stateroom forward and a larger saloon and galley aft).

Some well-known trawlers—The original trawler, the Grand Banks, is perhaps the most universally recognized trawler brand name, and it has earned an excellent reputation. New 32-foot Grand Banks are available from the low $300,000s, and a good supply of used trawlers from various manufacturers exists with prices well under $100,000. The majority of trawlers, including the Grand Banks line, have traditionally been built in Asia. Nordhavn, Krogen, and Sabreline are other names well known to trawler enthusiasts.

MOTORYACHTS

Motoryachts are the largest and most luxurious powerboats. Few boats under 45 feet truly deserve the title, and custom-built, megamillion-dollar megayachts in the 150-foot range are still considered members of the motoryacht class. Many of the larger motoryachts are too large to be safely handled by a couple and require an experienced crew to be quartered and provisioned for in addition to the owners and their guests. With an almost unlimited budget to work with, naval architects have created many custom motoryachts which combine world cruise capability with virtually unrestrained opulence and comfort. Vessels produced in this category are built in such small numbers that individual boats can be highly customized as well. Most readers of this book will not begin their boating experiences on a motoryacht.

Common motoryacht examples—Not every boat in the motoryacht category is beyond the means of the merely wealthy. As usual, Bayliner offers one of the lower priced motoryachts available with a 4788 Motoryacht which the *1997 ABOS Marine Blue Book* lists at $343,000. More typically priced examples might be the Carver 455 listing at $448,000, the Mainship 47 at $510,000, the Sea Ray 550 Sedan Bridge at $798,000 and the Hatteras 65-foot Motoryacht at $1.75 million.

5

Hull Designs

Mの ORE THAN ANY OTHER single factor, the hull design of a powerboat dictates the type of boating you do. While there are hundreds of variations on each theme, hull designs in powerboats consist of three basic varieties: planing, displacement, and semi-displacement hulls.

PLANING HULLS

Planing hulls are designed to cause much of the boat to lift above the surface as the vessel's speed increases. Since air offers less resistance to travel than does water, less wetted surfaces reduce drag on the hull. Ski boats, racing craft, and many trailerable weekend cruisers rely on the planing principle to achieve maximum possible speed. Planing hulls use high-horsepower, high-rpm engines (frequently gasoline burning). They quite commonly incorporate a series of adjustable underwater flaps known as trim tabs. Trim tabs are used to level out and control the ride of a planing boat as it flies through the water's surface. In the search for greater lift and less resistance, manufacturers are constantly experimenting with combinations of steps, ridges, reverse curves, and strategically placed channels below the waterlines of planing hulls. For boaters requiring maximum possible speed, a planing hull allows a boat to cover the greatest distance in a minimum of time.

The disadvantages of planing hulls include high fuel consumption, high engine noise levels, and a tendency to bounce and slam across the waves in seas any heavier than a light to moderate chop. Boaters operating a boat at planing speeds learn to keep a sharp eye for logs or debris floating in the water. A log that would simply make an alarming thump against the hull at 8 knots might very easily hole a boat if struck at 20 knots. The characteristics of a planing hull can, in some designs, actually make the craft a little less seaworthy at slower speeds, when the vessel is not up on plane. Planing hull boaters also keep a sharp eye on the weather and use the higher speed of their vessels to get to shelter quickly in the event of rough weather.

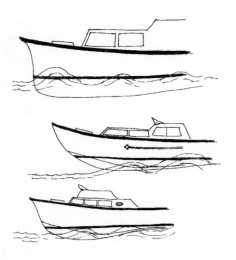

Displacement, planing and semi-displacement hulls.

There is a practical limit to how large a superstructure can be placed on a planing hull without resorting to multi-hull configurations (such as a catamaran) to support the weight, or having to use monster engines to get an extra heavy vessel up on plane. Because of the generally shallower draft, planing hull vessels tend to be affected more by winds than by currents when maneuvering at slow speeds (as when navigating through a marina or docking).

DISPLACEMENT HULLS

Displacement hulls are typically found on the largest, most seaworthy vessels and rarely, if ever, on a trailer boat. Displacement hulls feature deep drafts, usually with a full-length keel to improve directional stability. The transom on a displacement hull is typically completely above the normal waterline, thereby reducing the effect of strong following seas that might create steering difficulty or even broaching (turning sideways) in heavy weather. Displacement hulls tend to plow through rather than bounce over wakes and choppy seas. They can support more superstructure above the waterline than any other single-hull design, and are most commonly powered by diesel engines that emphasize high torque output at a lower rpm. As the construction of a displacement hull requires a larger amount of materials and labor, it is more expensive than a planing or semi-displacement configuration on a vessel of the same length. The ride of a displacement hull is more stable than the ride of a planing hull, and it is easier to move around the boat and hold a conversation while underway. Displacement hulls often achieve impressive fuel economy when considered from a gallons-per-hour perspective, but will be the slowest hull design in any given size category due to the drag created by the large mass of hull in the water.

Hull speed

Naval architects refer to hull speed when they discuss the speed potential of a boat's design. It is computed by multiplying 1.35 times the square root of the boat's waterline. Hull speed is the speed at which the hull design itself begins to resist traveling any faster. It can be as little as 5 or 6 knots on a displacement-hull pleasure craft, and it would be unusual to have a displacement hull speed of over 10 or 11. It is possible to push a vessel beyond hull speed by equipping it with monster engines and leaning heavily on the throttle, but most old salts (who seem to comprise a high percentage of the boaters gravitating to a displacement-hull craft) are likely to enjoy the passage as much as the arrival at a destination. They are willing to accept the slowest type of hull by virtue of its superior sea-keeping abilities. Single engines are very common on displacement hulls. Unless adorned with a mammoth superstructure, displacement hulls are more affected by tide or current than by normal winds when cruising or docking.

SEMI-DISPLACEMENT HULLS

Semi-displacement hulls are fairly common in medium-sized powerboats of 30—45 feet. The design goal of a semi-displacement hull is to incorporate some of the speed of planing hulls with some of the seaworthiness of displacement varieties. Depending on design variations, some semi-displacement hulls behave more like a true planing or displacement craft than others. Some semi-displacement hulls may even have trim tabs, while others may feature a modified keel design. Many semi-displacement hulls will have small steps built into them like planing hulls, to encourage greater lift as speeds increase. At the upper end of the speed range, some semi-displacement hulls may actually put little or none of the hull clear of the water. But in general the waterline will move down the hull enough to significantly reduce wetted surface and thereby reduce aquatic resistance.

Semi-displacement hulls are powered by either gasoline or diesel engines, with twin-engine configurations common. With large gasoline engines, semi-displacement hulls can achieve impressive speeds of 25 knots or more, but skippers who operate larger vessels at such speeds will spend a significant portion of their time, not to mention their family fortune, at the fuel dock. Semi-displacement hulls are a good choice for boaters who feel the need to break the 9-knot barrier, but want a larger, more open-water boat than a true planing hull.

BOWS

The design of a boat's bow has a great effect on its ability to either achieve maximum speed or withstand heavy sea conditions. Boats built for speed will feature a bow with as little wind resistance as possible, often fairly low to the water. While making the boat more aerodynamic, such a design does little to keep the deck dry when splashing through a large wall of water. A vessel with a higher bow, flaring outward above the waterline, is more suited to absorb the shock of larger waves or wakes, and will have a tendency to direct much of the spray away from the boat when settling into a trough between waves. With displacement hulls, special attention is paid to designing an entry angle in the hull shape to allow the boat to make forward progress with as little initial water resistance as possible.

STERNS AND CHINES

Two other important aspects of hull design that bear on a boat's handling characteristics are whether the boat has a hard or soft chine, and the shape of the stern. The chine is where the boat's side meets the bottom. A hard chine has a definite angled or cornerlike appearance, and creates a flat plane of resistance to help control rolling motion when the hull is subjected to a beam sea. A soft chine has a more rounded, bowl-like shape that tends to continue to curve outward above the normal waterline. As a soft-chine boat rolls to either side, it relies on the increasing amount of wetted surface to create the buoyancy to help right the boat again. Sailboats are the epitome of a soft chine design. A hard chine will provide more resistance to rolling in the light to moderate seas prevailing when most pleasure boaters should venture out, but a seriously designed soft-chined craft with a low center of gravity might have its advantages in heavy storm conditions.

The shape of the stern dictates how much effect a following sea has on a boat's steering and stability underway. Most sterns on modern powerboats feature large, flat transoms to allow greater room in cockpits and aft cabins—creating a little "more boat for the buck" from many perspectives. These large transoms often have square corners which tend to catch a following sea. The result is that the stern gets pushed to either starboard or port and steering corrections must be made to stay on course and to avoid broaching into

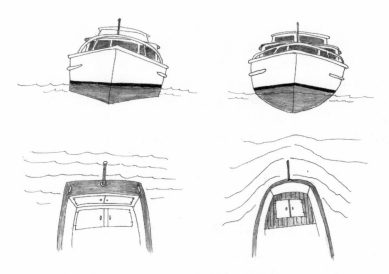

Hard chines, soft chines, square and rounded sterns.

the oncoming waves. A stern with a round shape or at least rounded corners allows following seas to pass under the transom with less effect on the boat's course and steering.

FREE LOCAL ADVICE

When pondering options of hull design (and most other nautical subjects as well), boat owners can be an excellent resource. Boaters you know will normally be happy to share their opinions about the advantages and disadvantages of their particular boats. Ask specific questions about how their boats handle in the conditions common to the local cruising area. Don't know any boaters? Not a problem. By heading down to the local dock and opening a conversation with a compliment about how great a boat looks, it's easy to strike up conversations with the majority of boaters. They never tire of the opportunity to pontificate on the particulars of their nautical pride and joy.

6

Hull Materials

HISTORICALLY, BOATS HAVE BEEN made from any number of materials including leather, steel, cement, aluminum, reeds, tree bark, bamboo, every type of wood (with the possible exception of petrified), plywood, and fiberglass. During the last half of the 20th century, the construction of pleasure boats changed from almost exclusively wood to almost exclusively fiberglass. Shoppers looking at new boats will see an all-fiberglass array except for the products of a few custom or semi-custom builders. When shopping for an older boat, you will find both wood and fiberglass options, with wooden boats being either traditional plank- or plywood-style construction.

PROS AND CONS OF WOOD

Simply because fiberglass technology is newer does not mean it is therefore superior in every aspect to wood. Wooden boat aficionados insist that wood is somehow "homier and warmer" than fiberglass, and many feel that a wooden hull absorbs engine vibrations better to create a quieter boat as well. Builders of fiberglass boats often rely on wooden cabin interiors and exterior trim pieces to increase the charm of their vessels (while owners of wooden boats are not usually seen rushing out to acquire

Wood versus fiberglass construction.

plastic trim pieces to dress up their craft). Wood is an organic material, subject to rot and decay. Fastidious maintenance will control or postpone the rotting process, but it cannot be eliminated entirely. Wooden boats operated in saltwater tend to maintain the integrity of the wood in their hull longer than freshwater wood boats, due to the preservative qualities of sea salt. Some freshwater wooden boaters have been known to keep a little rock salt in the bilge in an attempt to create the same preservative effect. Traditionally constructed wooden hulls incorporate a number of planks fastened with screws to underlying ribs. When a section of planking or even a rib begins to get soft from rot and decay it is possible to partially dismantle a wooden hull and replace the affected portions. Every so often a wooden-planked hull must be re-fastened in order to maintain structural integrity, with the screws used to hold the planking to the ribs being completely replaced. Wood in the marine environment must be protected by either paint or varnish to repel rot-promoting moisture, and this protective coating must be relentlessly maintained and renewed.

Beware of "Wood Boat-itis"

Wooden boats are typically older than comparable fiberglass models and some large, old wooden boats can be available for purchase at what seems to be a bargain price. A prudent shopper will look past the "Wow!" factor at least far enough to realize that maintenance costs, in time and money, on a 20- to 50-year-old wooden hull are a significant factor. Some disclosures by sellers may mean little to an inexperienced boat buyer with palpitating heart and dollar signs in his or her eyes—and who might perhaps react, "So what if it needs to be hauled out and completely refastened, whatever that means. This boat's twice as big as anything else we've been able to consider buying!"

CHARACTERISTICS OF FIBERGLASS

When introduced, fiberglass was touted as a nearly miraculous boat-building material. Here at last was a material which could be formed into any number of curved surfaces, had high structural integrity, and was not subject to rot and decay. As fiberglass boats are now commonplace and have aged, some limitations have become apparent. Fiberglass boats are constructed by sandwiching together many layers of fiberglass cloth impregnated with resin to form a solid, plastic-like structure. As a boat ages, it is not uncommon for the fiberglass to delaminate and/or blister. Delamination can be cured by drilling into the affected area of small sections, injecting some resin-type compounds formulated for such repairs, and clamping the material back together until cured and resecured.

Blisters

On fiberglass boats, blisters can form on the outside of the hull below the waterline. Most blisters are gelcoat blisters which bubble up under the smooth upper layer of the fiberglass sandwich when water chemically reacts with certain elements of the fiberglass resin. Some hull experts advise that so long as a blister is confined to the gelcoat layer, it can be safely ignored. Another school of thought opines that any blistering must be dealt with immediately and decisively. Blisters can be cured by hauling the boat, grinding down the blister, drying the hull, filling, fairing, and re-gelcoating the affected area. The drying process can be lengthy, and a boat can be laid up for several weeks, resulting in a whopping yard bill.

Maintaining the Appearance of Fiberglass

The smooth, shiny gelcoat finish on a new boat must be cleaned and waxed regularly to prevent oxidization. On older fiberglass boats where the gelcoat has been allowed to become chalky to the point of no return, painting the boat with a top-quality yacht enamel is the only method to restore the appearance; and painting a 36-foot boat can cost as much as purchasing an economy car. Some manufacturers of upper-end yachts who can utilize virtually "perfect" molds actually paint the hulls at the time of initial construction rather than rely on gelcoat to create and maintain the beauty of their high-dollar product.

PLYWOOD AND FIBERGLASS COMPOSITES

Some boats are built with plywood covered with fiberglass, and some boats with fiberglass hulls have cabin structures built this way. Experience has shown that this combination is often more trouble prone than all-wood or all-fiberglass configurations. The hull of a boat flexes slightly when pounding through a head sea. It also expands or contracts with exposure to heat or moisture. Dissimilar materials react differently. When dissimilar materials are fastened together, internal stresses develop as a result. Plywood can begin to delaminate beneath the fiberglass. Any water trapped between the wood and the fiberglass layers will accelerate the process. Fiberglass-over-wood superstructures have been known to keep boat owners busy chasing rainwater leaks which can be difficult to find and cosmetically or even structurally damaging. For most boaters, all-wood or all-fiberglass construction is less prone to trouble than fiberglass bonded to plywood.

7

Engine Choices

ONE ENGINE OR TWO?

On most boats under 32 feet there is no debate on this issue. Small boats are typically built with only a single engine or in some cases no engine at all (leaving it up to the purchaser to supply an outboard power plant). Small single-engine boats are commonly an inboard/outboard design with the engine mounted below deck at the stern of the vessel connecting to a drive mechanism mounted on the transom. Steering is accomplished by turning the drive unit to starboard or port while underway, to power the stern in the opposite direction. Owners of such boats often report experiencing as many problems with the out-drive as with the engine itself, with comparable costs for maintenance and repair. By about 30 feet, nearly every manufacturer switches to an inboard-mounted engine and a fixed propeller, with steering accomplished by a movable rudder. Occasionally at about 32 feet and commonly at 36 feet and above, one of the decisions a boat buyer will consider is whether to select a boat with a single or dual engines.

Single-Engine Advantages

Single-engine vessels are less costly and time consuming to maintain than twin-engine, consuming fewer oil filters, zincs, hoses, belts, starters, alternators, etc. (not to mention less lubricating oil, gasoline, or diesel). In single-engine boats the engine is in the center of the hull. Since most hulls are deepest in the middle, the engine can be set a little lower in relationship to the waterline than an installation of two engines mounted equidistant from the centerline. Setting the engine lower can result in a more favorable angle at which the drive shaft protrudes through the hull, increasing propeller efficiency. An engine placed lower in the bilge may also improve balance and ballast characteristics of a boat. A single engine in the center of the hull can allow better access to both the starboard and port sides of the engine to facilitate routine servicing. And if it follows that an item more easily serviced will be serviced more often, a single-engine installation has a notable advantage in this respect. Single-engine installations achieve the best fuel economy. A single engine is often used in conjunction with an auxiliary engine that drives a generator and in some cases can be used to turn the prop shaft and allow a slow return to harbor, should the main engine fail. The disadvantages of a single engine include reduced close-quarters maneuverability (requiring the development of some docking and boat-handling skills unique to single-engine skippers) and the reliance on a single power plant for motive power.

Why Twin Engines Are Popular

Redundancy is a major safety factor on a boat, especially a vessel operating far offshore. A prudent skipper has a contingency plan to deal with the failure of any major system on board. Nothing could be more redundant than an extra engine with which to limp back to the dock in case the other engine should fail. Single-engine boaters achieve a measure of redundancy by keeping an adequate supply of spare parts (rubber v-belts, raw-water pump impellers, spark plugs, distributor cap and rotor, etc.) aboard to effect emergency repairs of common failures at sea. Boaters should keep an adequate selection of tools and spare parts aboard a boat at all times and develop an understanding of elementary mechanics, but single-engine boaters must be particularly prepared to make minor repairs while underway. Some diesel engine fans could argue that a single diesel engine is as reliable as two gasoline engines, but even if true, two diesel engines would be more reliable yet.

Adding a second engine offers a few advantages beyond simply having spare propulsion potential. A boat with twin engines will usually achieve greater speed than the same hull with a single screw, but in practical terms the speed will never double. The weight of the second engine will cause the hull to settle a little deeper in the water, increasing the wetted surface and creating additional drag. The concept of hull speed applies, regardless of the number of engines, and a boat with displacement hull characteristics that might cruise at 9 knots with a single engine will often do no more than 11 or 12 knots with twin engines while consuming twice the fuel per hour. A second engine will be of no particular advantage under many of the conditions that lead to mechanical failure on a boat. A boater out of fuel (or with contaminated fuel) or a boater with dead batteries will be just as stuck with two engines as with one.

Maneuverability

For many boaters, the primary advantage of twin engines is the additional flexibility of close-quarters movement when docking. With one engine in forward and the other in reverse, it is possible to turn a boat on the spot. Without the addition of a bow thruster even the most highly skilled single-engine boater would have a difficult time duplicating the maneuvers of the average twin-engine operator. Should the hydraulic or mechanical steering system fail (a very rare occurrence), a twin-engine boat can steer by adjusting the speed and the direction of the engines. Twin-engine boats can be steered more easily in reverse than a single-engine vessel as well.

Bow and Stern Thrusters

Single-engine craft that are frequently operated in crowded conditions such as busy marinas and locks, or occasionally operated by a single individual without benefit of a deck crew, will benefit from the addition of a bow thruster. A bow thruster consists of a single, reversible propeller mounted athwartship below the waterline in a tunnel running through the bow, or two propellers with one facing starboard and the other port. On boats under 40 feet, most bow thrusters are electrically driven, while on larger vessels hydraulic units are more common. The bow thruster's function is to move the bow of the vessel to port or starboard independently of any influence from the prop and rudder in the stern. When docking or undocking either in windy conditions or when single handed, a bow thruster can help a boater avoid some embarrassing moments.

In addition to, or sometimes instead of a bow thruster, many boaters have installed stern thrusters. A stern thruster operates under the same principle as a bow thruster, but mounted in the stern. It pushes the stern to starboard or port without any of the forward or reverse momentum which would result from using the rudder and prop. With both bow and stern thrusters aboard, a single-engine boater with the benefit of a little practice can practically move a vessel sideways into or out of a crowded dock.

With bow and stern thrusters, a skillful skipper can move a boat almost sideways into a slip.

Cost and Resale

A factor that cannot be overlooked is the effect on purchase cost and resale value of a second engine. New diesel engines typically sell for prices that represent many months' income for most boat owners, and gasoline engines can be costly as well. A second engine could make a sizable difference in the monthly boat payment, requiring other compromises in order to make a boat affordable. Some of the cost of a second engine will be recovered when and if the boat is resold, as used twin-engine boats also bring more dollars than similarly sized and equipped used single-engine vessels.

GAS OR DIESEL?

When shopping for a small day cruiser or runabout, it is unusual to see anything other than gasoline engines. Boats in the 50-foot and over range will almost certainly be powered by diesel. Between 26 and 50 feet, the choices include both gasoline- and diesel-powered boats, with many manufacturers offering gasoline engines as standard equipment and charging extra for diesel engines as an optional upgrade.

Gas Engine Characteristics

Gasoline engines typically operate at higher rpms than diesels, which can be desirable when the function of the engine is to turn a propeller. By virtue of these higher rpms as well as a much lighter weight, gasoline engines will often achieve greater speed than diesel in the same hull. Most boaters drive gasoline-powered cars or trucks, so there is something comfortable and familiar about the concept of a gasoline engine. In the event of mechanical problems a boater would perhaps feel a little more comfortable attempting to troubleshoot the situation. Gasoline engines are much cheaper to buy, new or used, than diesels. The cost advantage is offset by the much shorter life expectancy of gasoline engines. Twenty-five hundred hours on marine engines is equivalent to operating a vehicle on land for 150,000 miles at 60 mph uphill. A gasoline engine with that many hours could soon be a candidate for replacement or rebuilding. Prudent skippers will overhaul a gasoline engine at even fewer hours for safety and reliability or because some mechanical bad luck has befallen it. While there is no scientifically established standard for the number of engine hours a boater will accumulate in a year, 150 to 400 engine hours covers the range of annual usage for most weekend and vacation boaters.

Gasoline is highly flammable, and in an improperly vented engine room the fumes can create an explosion hazard. To be certain that vapors don't accumulate, gasoline boats must operate bilge blowers before initially starting the engines and when running at anything less than cruising speeds. A well-equipped gasoline-powered boat will have an electronic "sniffer" in the engine room to set off an alarm before gasoline fumes reach a potentially explosive level. The sniffer may automatically activate the bilge blower motors as well. Since gasoline engines rely on the introduction of an electric spark into the combustion chamber to ignite the fuel-air mixture, gas engines have an entire ignition system of electrical coils, points, condensers, wires, distributors, caps, rotors, etc. These electrical ignition components are not always completely happy in the marine environment and must be constantly maintained to assure optimum engine reliability and performance. Virtually every fuel dock offers gasoline for sale, but only the larger facilities usually carry diesel fuel as well.

Older gasoline engines are usually carbureted, while the more modern engines are fuel injected. Fuel-injected gasoline engines are more efficient and somewhat safer than their carbureted equivalents.

Diesel Engines Characteristics

Diesel engines develop more torque than gasoline engines of similar displacement. So while a gasoline engine might turn a prop at a faster speed, a diesel engine can turn a larger prop.

The diesel combustion system is very simple: air is compressed in the cylinder to a ratio approximately twice as high as in a gasoline engine; the rapid molecular motion of the highly squeezed air creates a super-heated condition into which diesel fuel is injected. Since the heat for combustion is created without electric spark, diesel engines have no need for an ignition system, and there is no need to perform ignition system tune-ups. To create and contain the exceptionally high compression ratios, a diesel engine is built on a more mammoth scale. Thicker engine blocks help dissipate heat more evenly, and heavier-duty cranks and bearings help prolong engine life as well. It is not unusual for a well-maintained marine diesel to achieve a service life of 10,000 hours or more.

All diesel engines are fuel injected, and higher-horsepower diesels are turbo charged as well. Boat shoppers who may have had an unhappy experience with a turbo-charged gasoline automobile engine back in the '80s (when Detroit was peddling four-cylinder turbo-charged engines as an alternative to larger-displacement six and eight cylinders) will be gratified to know that the mechanical dynamics of a diesel engine are far more compatible with the concept of turbo charging. The majority of turbo chargers on marine engines operate in an extremely reliable fashion. Under normal circumstances, diesel fumes present no risk of explosion.

Fuel economy can be outstanding with diesels. A large twin-engined boat that could easily burn 50–60 gallons of gasoline per hour might operate on as little as 15–20 gallons per hour of diesel or less. Since the gasoline-powered boat is probably traveling faster, a small portion of the difference is recovered by fewer hours on the water to reach the same destination. Some single-diesel trawler-style boats achieve eight- or nine-knot speeds while burning as little as 2 gallons of diesel fuel per hour.

Diesel may incompletely combust in an engine operating cold and create more visible exhaust smoke until the engine reaches sufficient operating temperature. Many normally excellent-running diesel engines can create a small cloud in the marina when first started from a cold condition. Diesel boaters spend more time scrubbing the exhaust soot off the transom. From an air pollution standpoint, diesel emits more visible smoke per gallon burned than does gasoline, but this is generally offset by the reduced numbers of gallons which are used. As the market fluctuates, there will be times when diesel is cheaper per gallon than gasoline and other times when gasoline will cost less.

REPOWERING AT PURCHASE

On occasion, the purchaser of a used boat is aware that the vessel will need to be repowered. The most common scenario consists of worn-out gasoline engines which need almost immediate replacement. Many boaters take this opportunity to consider replacing the gasoline engines with diesels. Such a decision shouldn't be automatic or undertaken lightly, and a lot of input from the vessel's manufacturer and/or designer as well as from various suppliers of potential diesel power plants will need to be carefully evaluated first.

NO RIGHT ANSWER

Gas or diesel? Certainly the relative merits of the two engines are among the most commonly debated topics in boating. Diesel engines are more costly to acquire, have a higher resale value, and cost less per hour to operate than gas. No single answer is right for every boat and every boater, but the larger and more "shiplike" the vessel, the greater the probability that it will be diesel-powered. A gasoline engine proponent was recently overheard remarking to the owner of a similar boat with diesel engines, "You'll never save enough fuel to offset the higher cost of those diesels!" To which the diesel boater replied, "One set of diesel engines lasting me the rest of my boating life is a lot less expensive than replacing gas engines three or four times." They were probably both right.

8

The Budget Process

WHERE TO FIND BOAT MONEY

A boat takes shape in the imagination. Prior to actively shopping for the boat, it is useful to identify an amount of disposable income available each month for boating. For most boaters, some of it will be money currently being spent for something else. Since it's not possible to be two places at once, some of the family entertainment budget which has customarily been spent for sporting events, nights at the pizza parlor, movies and popcorn, weekends spent in a hotel at the shore (being envious of folks who already have a boat), and trips to the video rental store can be painlessly transferred to boating. Many families boat quite handsomely on the same amount of money that others spend on motor homes or owning a summer cabin. A boat is like a waterfront property with an ever changing view. Some of the money can actually come from Uncle Sam. Under the current tax laws, a boat with a galley and a head often qualifies as a second home and money spent for interest on a boat loan is then deductible from your income before calculating taxes due. (Check with your accountant.) Once a figure has been set that the family budget can withstand, a few allowances need to be made before any conclusions can be drawn about the amount of money available each month to service a boat loan.

MISCELLANEOUS EXPENSES

Unless your preference is for a trailerable boat, the first expense to consider will be moorage. While rates vary from region to region, it may not be easy to find decent moorage for much under $8–10 per foot per month. Add utilities (shore power, etc.) and any applicable taxes, and it is not difficult to approach $350–400 per month for space to dock a medium-sized powerboat. Trailer boaters are not necessarily immune from similar charges, as many residential neighborhoods prohibit parking boats in driveways, and a storage lot will need to be rented. (Not to mention the megathousand-dollar four-wheel-drive truck many trailer boaters buy to tow and launch the vessel!) Insurance will run several hundred or more dollars a year, so a $30–50 per month allocation might be a realistic expectation. Soaps, polishes, waxes, miscellaneous spare parts for routine repairs and so forth can consume $100 a month, and a prudent boat owner will set aside fifty cents per engine operating hour for lubricating oil and filters. Every fifty engine hours is not too frequent to schedule an oil change, for as the adage states, "Oil is the cheapest thing you'll ever put into an engine." After spending a few hundred or more annually for haul out and bottom painting, it's not unusual to allocate a regular monthly budget in excess of $500, before making the loan payment or leaving the dock. The older the boat, the greater should be a boater's expectation that higher than average expenses for maintenance and repairs will be required.

Fuel

Fuel costs need to be taken into account as well. Should a boater's taste run toward large, high-speed vessels with two big-block gasoline engines, $200 or more per weekend would not be a high fuel bill. At the other extreme, eight-knot single-engine diesel boats with a decent fuel capacity may literally only need to stop at a fuel dock once or twice a year, with perhaps $20–30 or less being consumed on a two-day cruise.

FIRST LAW OF BOATING ECONOMICS

It is not wise to attempt to boat on the cheap. Purchasing a low-priced craft of questionable seaworthiness and allowing it to further deteriorate through continued financial neglect may seem like fiscal prudence to some, but the first law of boating economics still applies: "The less spent to get afloat, the more needed to stay afloat." Few people would consider charging down the highway in a motor vehicle with bad brakes, broken springs, questionable steering, and an over-heating engine. Yet the seagoing equivalents of such vehicles are frequently seen being boarded in marinas by boaters who, unintentionally, plan to place themselves and their families in harm's way. If a cheap old car breaks, the driver and passengers can at least get out and walk. By allocating sufficient financial resources to obtain and maintain a decent boat (not necessarily an extravagant boat), purchasing and using the craft will be a far more enjoyable experience.

PRICE RANGE

After deducting the monthly maintenance, moorage, and fuel costs the remainder of the budget will service the

The sea going equivalent of a "cheap old car."

boat loan. Of course, there are those boaters who can pay cash. But for the rest of us, a few minutes on the phone with the bank will give an idea of the prevailing interest rates and amortizations for boat loans and assist in identifying a realistic amount which can be borrowed for a boat. Adding whatever cash is available for a down-payment will indicate the appropriate price range of vessels to consider.

AMORTIZATION CHART

The monthly payment required to retire a loan of $1,000 at various interest rates and number of contract years is calculated by multiplying the payments shown by the number of thousands of dollars borrowed. Terms exceeding 15 years for used boats or 20 years for new boats are unusual.

ANNUAL PERCENTAGE RATES

Years	7%	8%	9%	10%	11%
5	19.80	20.27	20.75	21.24	21.74
10	11.61	12.13	12.66	13.21	13.77
15	8.99	9.55	10.14	10.74	11.36
20	7.75	8.36	9.00	9.65	10.32

DEPRECIATION

While certainly not a cash expense, an item for consideration when contemplating the economics of owning a powerboat is the depreciation. For a new boat, in particular, depreciation takes an immediate toll on net worth the moment the engine starts. Various boats depreciate more or less rapidly than others, but no knowledgeable buyer of a used boat would ever pay as much as (or even close to) the price of the same boat in brand new condition. Depreciation is inevitable.

In the broadest terms, five-year-old boats resell for about 60 percent of their current retail replacement cost. Inflation can disguise depreciation, creating an appearance that at least in nominal dollars very little depreciation actually takes place. For example; a new powerboat is purchased at the beginning of year one for $100,000. The retail cost of the boat escalates 5 percent per year for five years to $127,630. If the boat were resold at the end of year five for 60 percent of the current replacement cost, it would fetch $76,580, or only a little over $23,000 less than when purchased new.

Ten-year-old boats in excellent condition will generally sell for about 40 percent of the replacement cost for a similar new boat, and bristol 20-year-old boats will often bring about 25 percent of the replacement cost. During decades of high monetary inflation, some used boats appear to appreciate in price, even though the actual market value of the dollars involved continues to decline.

BOATS AND MONEY

Shorebound friends (usually seething with envy) often scold boaters with such clichés as "a boat is a hole in the water into which one pours money!" and have been known to ask, "How do you justify spending money on a boat?" Some of the happiest boaters around have been heard to reply, "We don't justify it! We just spend it, forget about it, and enjoy life... a lot!"

9

Charter's a Starter

AFTER CAREFUL CONSIDERATION and some preliminary visits to local marinas, the style, price range,
approximate size, and general configuration of the boat
with the most acceptable group of compromises should
begin to become apparent.

An excellent way to try on a particular type of boat is
to charter one for at least a weekend. Chartering is not
inexpensive, but then again neither is purchasing a boat
which turns out to be wrong for you.

SOME EXPERIENCE REQUIRED

A completely inexperienced boater will not be allowed to
just climb aboard and take off with what could easily be a
quarter-million-dollar vessel. He or she may need a friend
who does have sufficient experience (or even hire a
licensed captain to operate the boat). The novice then garners whatever education possible and perhaps spends some
time behind the wheel in open water under close supervi-
sion. A responsible charter operator will make certain that
even an experienced boater knows the idiosyncracies of a
particular vessel and will be capable of safely docking and
maneuvering it without damage. So during the check-out
session of a chartering experience it is possible to learn a lot

about how quickly a boat responds to helm and rudder, how much of a factor windage will be, and so forth.

At-Dock Charters

In the absence of having anybody available to operate a chartered boat, it may be possible (particularly during the off season) to arrange for an at-dock charter. Spending a rainy dockside weekend aboard a boat may stress all but the most devoted domestic relationships, but it will help clarify the rewards and difficulties that cruising aboard a particular boat might represent.

SEA TRIAL MAY NOT BE ENOUGH

When making an offer to purchase a boat, it is customary to require that the owner of the boat make it available for sea trial. A typical sea trial is a fairly short, out-around-the-mid-channel-buoy-and-back sort of affair and is ordinarily not undertaken until a prospective buyer has made a conditional commitment. During sea trial the broker or the owner of the boat is often selling, nonstop, every whistle, bell, gadget, and geegaw aboard. It may be difficult to concentrate on the vessel's handling characteristics or experience enough variables in wind and sea conditions during a short run. Ever buy a car after a 10-minute test drive that you might not have selected had you rented it for a couple of days first?

ALTERNATIVES TO CHARTERING

An alternative to chartering is available to those who have friends that currently own boats: snag an invitation for at least a short cruise or two. After a couple of cruises on different boats it should be easy to develop an informed opinion about the 34-foot express cruiser, the 38-foot aft-cabin model, and the 36-foot pilot-house trawler. Some careful politicking could be called for, lest one boating friend or another become upset that you have selected someone else's boat! A couple of hours spent helping a skipper clean up after the cruise and a contribution toward fuel and other expenses is considered good etiquette among nautical guests. One can successfully purchase a boat without chartering first, but it won't hurt and may help significantly.

Time-Share Boating

In many communities it is possible to participate in time-share boating where a number of different boats are available for occasional use by the participants. Paying a monthly rental fee allows the boating family to use a certain boat a few days a month, subject to schedule coordination with the other time-share members. While most plans call for a minimum commitment of six months to a year, it may be possible during that time to transfer to a couple of different boats and sample a variety of hull types, sizes, and power options.

10

The Value of a Broker

So, AFTER CAREFUL ANALYSIS and introspection, a cursory preview of the marketplace, a hopefully realistic budgeting session, and possibly a couple of boat rides on charter boats or as the guest of some friends, you have narrowed the choices down to no more than a couple of categories of boats. You've maybe even thought specifically about a brand name or builder. It's time to begin selecting a boat, which can begin by selecting a broker.

BROKER'S ROLE WHEN SHOPPING USED

Finding the right yacht broker is very important when shopping for a used boat. Like real estate agencies, most yacht brokerages share their inventory listings with each other and belong to multiple-listing organizations which can make boats available literally worldwide. If you are lucky enough to encounter a broker or salesperson genuinely interested in helping in the acquisition of a boat reflecting your needs and desires, a salesperson with whom you have a rapport, it is often possible to ask that individual to assist with your purchase of a used vessel even if the inventory and in-house listings of this particular brokerage do not contain just the right boat at the moment. A couple of key questions: Does the broker seem to be a careful listener and make an effort to show you boats that make sense for you, or does he or she seem to be pushing a boat which clearly isn't what you're interested in? Is the salesperson more interested in helping you make decisions or in forcing decisions upon you?

STAY LOCAL WHEN BUYING NEW

If shopping for a new boat, a buyer may be stuck with the local brokerage which has an exclusive franchise to represent Squiddiddle Yachts. The advantage of the local broker representing Squiddiddle is that there should be no excuse for having any less than a perfect knowledge and understanding of the product represented, and it is prudent to have a working relationship with the company that may be arranging any warranty repairs or adjustments on a new boat. A buyer who selects a new Squiddiddle may feel compelled to check out of town for a comparison price in order to be confident of making a favorable deal on the boat.

In the larger scheme of boat ownership, if a prospective buyer elects to purchase new, it could well be worth an extra couple of percent in the final price to do business with the local vendor. (Given the opportunity, the local dealer might be willing to meet an out-of-town quote anyway.) When service is required it is so much more pleasant to be treated as an important, priority customer whose future business is worth cultivating than as the "damned cheapskate who drove 300 miles, cost us the deal, saved almost nothing, and will probably be an even bigger pain when it comes to having the boat serviced!" With a busy holiday weekend looming, it is somehow gratifying to have any required servicing performed with your boat being scheduled ahead of the out-of-town bargain hunters rather than behind the loyal locals.

Ask the Grapevine

Friends or acquaintances who have recently purchased a boat may be able to direct you to (or away from, as the case may be) various brokers in the community. While it may be helpful to consider this free advice, there is a good deal of personal chemistry involved in effective communication: the broker who is extremely helpful to one buyer may have a difficult time with another.

"FOR SALE BY OWNER?"

It is also possible to shop for a used boat "for sale by owner." A buyer needs to be particularly wary when dealing with a private seller. Deliberate misinformation and outright ripoffs perpetrated by established businesses are usually addressable by some government entity or another. When a business commits a fraud, local regulators can be quick to respond. If John Q. Public defrauds John X. Public out of several thousand dollars through either outright ignorance or some devious chicanery, it is probably a one-time event. Therefore it can be hard to bring any official pressure to bear on a dishonest private seller. Private disputes usually wind up in civil court, where the attorneys usually emerge as the only genuine winners. Most private individuals selling a boat aren't motivated to do so by the altruistic notion of offering a cheaper price. In general they hope to get just as much as a broker and save themselves (not the buyer) the cost of the commission. A boat is far more difficult to find a buyer for than a used car and sometimes more difficult to sell than a house, so a very high percentage of used boats for sale are represented by brokerages.

When buying a first powerboat, the value of a knowledgeable broker will ordinarily far exceed the commission paid. Yes, the majority of private sellers will be more or less honest and there are some brokers who might be unethical at times. But the licensing and legal establishments and a broker's self-interested desire to perpetuate business and reputation make the use of such an experienced agent a wise course for the first-time buyer.

PART TWO

Inspecting
the Primary
Systems

A T THIS POINT WE'LL BEGIN to examine some of the more important aspects of a boat to acquaint a first-time buyer with what the various systems consist of and how to make somewhat informed casual observations. We'll categorize these items which are not easily changed or replaced and are fundamental aspects of the boat's design and construction as "primary systems."

THE LIMITATIONS OF ADVERTISING

Boat for Sale. 38 Ft. Buckingham Sundeck. New canvas and bottom paint, 10 ft inflatable dinghy, GPS, radar, and 10 disc CD changer. Twin 454's. $XXXXXX. Phone..........

Most privately placed ads and a large portion of brokerage ads contain little useful information or tend to emphasize fluff over function—not surprising when one considers that the function of the ad isn't to sell the boat but to generate phone calls and allow the seller to make appointments with potential prospects. It shouldn't be surprising either that many people shopping for their first powerboat suffer from advertising-induced confusion regarding what aspects of a vessel are of greatest importance. Even when attempting to carefully inspect a boat, first-time buyers can have little understanding of what they're actually looking at. Items or conditions which are important get overlooked or ignored.

THE PRELIMINARY SURVEY

Used boats are ordinarily bought and sold subject to inspection by an independent surveyor. Every boat buyer should insist on a survey when making an offer, especially when purchasing a used boat. Lending institutions will require a survey in order to substantiate value when calculating the maximum loan available on a previously owned vessel. Surveys have even been performed on new boats, turning up such things as wires that have been misrouted, installed items not properly secured, parts installed that are less than spec. No inspection by a boat buyer will ever substitute for a good survey. But since the costs of hauling the boat out of the water and hiring the surveyor (two items that get up into the hundreds of dollars very quickly) are traditionally borne by the prospective purchaser, discovering conditions which are serious problems or shortcomings in a boat prior to making an "offer subject to survey" can save a good deal of time and frustration as well as cash. The surveyor can render an expert opinion regarding the condition of the hull and the equipment but will be operating under the assumption that the buyer has reached an independent conclusion that the boat, if sound, is suitable in the first place.

THE BENEFIT OF VOCABULARY

Many items found aboard a boat and much of the vocabulary used to describe them are unique to boating. More than a few novice boaters have nodded as if completely understanding while listening to a discourse that might as well have been "the flibbity gibbet has been moved aft to accommodate a larger hockum snocker, and the framus has been refitted with a fresh diogenator upgraded to mofligander standards." Two of the traditional difficulties when trying to communicate on any technical subject is the assumption of one party that "everybody knows what I'm talking about," and the reluctance of another party to appear underinformed which may prevent him from stating, "Could you repeat it in layman's terms?" Becoming familiar with some of the major systems aboard a powerboat will be of immeasurable assistance in conducting informative discussions with a seller.

11

Start with the "Heart"

I F YOU WERE TO VISIT a doctor to have your health
assessed and the doctor spent most of the appointment
examining toe nails and eyelashes, it might be difficult to
develop a strict confidence in the comprehensiveness of
the exam. You might ask, "Doc, how about my heart? It's
the single organ that will kill me quick if it stops working!"
Boat shoppers often act like the absent minded physician
described above. It isn't unusual for prospective buyers to
concentrate on the upholstery, the electronics, the appliances in the galley, and whether or not there's a tub in the
head, while completely forgetting to examine the engine
room where the "heart" of any powerboat is contained.

While there's very little point in thoroughly examining a prospective acquisition if it is somehow unsuitable,
once an initially favorable impression is established, it
becomes appropriate to begin a hard scrutiny of the nuts
and bolts of a vessel. It is of course impossible to determine
how well a boat will run by visual inspection alone, but
certain things seen or not seen in the engine room can give
some indications of what to expect. The engine room contains the largest concentration of equipment on a boat,
much of which can be almost prohibitively costly to
replace. How well it all works will not really be evident

until sea trial, and sea trial won't occur in most instances until there's a conditional offer and deposit. A boat buyer must initially rely on what he sees to draw preliminary conclusions about the mechanical condition of a vessel.

THE ENGINE ROOM

Access to the engine room is typically down through the rear deck on boats with a cockpit, or through the cabin sole on boats with engines mounted more amidships. On larger vessels, some owners enjoy the luxury of walk-in engine rooms with ample space for servicing the machinery, and perhaps even tool-storage lockers and a workbench. Unless you plan to hire out all of the mechanical work, you have to envision a few afternoons each year (possibly on hands and knees) changing oil, filters, zincs, and other routine tasks. Accessibility is an important consideration. On twin-engine installations, some builders have configured the engine assemblies to maximize ease of access to dipsticks, filters, etc., while others have not.

Lighting

Adequate light in the engine room is a necessity. The lack of it will require the dexterity to juggle a flashlight as well as a wrench or a screwdriver at the same time. A 120-volt light system to back up the 12-volt fixtures is a desirable luxury, as most routine maintenance will occur when the boat is docked and connected to shore power. While it can be difficult on medium-sized and smaller boats to keep even industrial light bulbs from vibrating themselves into a useless state, one or two 120-volt outlets into which a boater can connect a portable "trouble light" will serve as well as a permanent fixture. The portability of the unit will allow light to be concentrated on particular portions of an engine undergoing adjustment or repair. There is some wisdom in

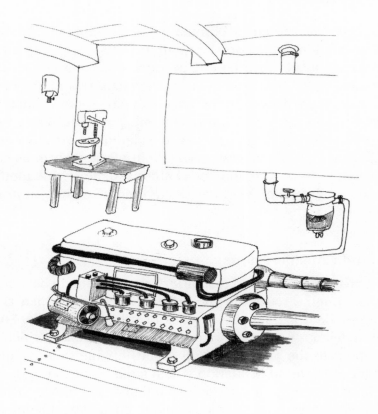

On larger vessels, some owners enjoy the luxury of a walk-in engine room.

bringing a small flashlight along during the initial examination of a powerboat, and rubber kneepads are found aboard many vessels without room to stand in the engine room, for reasons which can quickly become painfully apparent to boaters who haven't acquired the kneepads yet.

Ventilation

Gasoline-powered boats should, by virtue of their design alone, have exceptionally good engine-room ventilation with power-driven blowers to eliminate the possibility of explosive accumulations of vapors. Ventilation is also very important on diesel boats, since no engine runs well if starved for air, but on a diesel boat ventilation of the engine room and bilge areas does not need to be fan forced. Engine-room ventilation will remove the acidic fumes that are produced when wet-cell batteries recharge, and it is considered universally desirable to keep as much engine smell out of the interior as possible. Adequate ventilation can help make the engine room a cooler and fresher working environment on hot summer afternoons.

Sound Considerations

If a boat has had sound insulation installed, it will be visible in the engine room, on the walls and ceiling, which is of course the underside of the deck or cabin sole above. Look for a layer of material ordinarily ⅜" or thicker which is resilient to the touch and will absorb engine noises. Some boats use a sound insulation which looks more like acoustic ceiling tile. Sound insulation will enhance any power boat—when can you remember a complaint about a boat being too quiet?—but many have been constructed with either an inadequate amount or none. Should you find a boat without adequate sound insulation it might be advisable to carefully scrutinize whether other shortcuts have been taken. Boats built with bulkheads close enough forward and aft of the engine(s) to contain engine noise in a smaller space operate more quietly than vessels where the engine noise can spread unchecked through a more open area below decks.

"Oily" Warning

Engine-room surfaces should not be greasy or oily unless there's a problem with the engine, such as bad crankcase ventilation, or a lot of sloppy mechanical work has occurred there. Either scenario could be cause for some concern. A marine engine and transmission should ordinarily be much cleaner than the engines found under the hoods of most automobiles. Auto engines can become dirty from splashing through mud puddles and the constant exposure to general road scum, but no such problems exist on a boat. Any oil or grease accumulating on the exterior of a marine engine has either been spilled there when adding fluids to the machinery or has leaked through a gasket or seal. There must be no trace of fuel residue around the fuel lines, fuel pump, carburetor, or fuel injectors. Locations which appear dry but have collected a lot of dirt may have leaked in the past.

Looking for Spares

An excellent clue to the maintenance habits of a boat's current owner is the presence or absence of spares in the engine room. Mechanically conscientious skippers will always have a case of engine oil, a spare oil filter or two, a spare drive belt, a grease gun, a couple of spare fuel filters, minor tune-up parts and spark plugs (for gas engines), a few pencil zincs, and so forth stowed somewhere aboard, most often in the engine room. If these items are aboard, it is more than likely because the present owner is mechanically astute enough to consider them important.

VISUALLY EXAMINING THE ENGINE

Oil and Fluids

If you thought to bring a paper towel or a rag (and only with the permission of the present owner or broker), a quick pull of the engine and gearbox dipsticks on a used boat can speak volumes to the knowledgeable shopper. Dirty, black, gritty oil in an engine is a problem from two aspects. The

first is that it has been allowed to get into a deplorable condition in the first place, and the second is that the present
owner is blasé enough about the situation to market the
boat in that state without regard for the importance of clean
oil. If the boat is using multiweight detergent oil, it will get
dark very quickly after an oil change but should not be tar-
like or gritty. In most engines where regular oil changes
have been performed, straight SAE 30- or 40-weight oil
should remain fairly transparent on the stick for 20 to 30
operating hours after an oil change. It can be determined
what type of oil is being used in an engine if there are a few
unopened containers aboard. While the science behind the
practice is often debated, many experienced boaters are
reluctant to switch the brand of oil being used in an engine.
Some convincing arguments have been advanced against
switching back and forth between single-viscosity and the
high-detergent multi-viscosity oils. A prudent practice is to
follow the engine manufacturer's recommendation regarding the type and viscosity of oil.

Marine transmission fluid should never smell burnt,
appear foamy, or be anything but a very transparent,
though probably pink- or red-colored liquid. Obviously,
both the engine and transmission dipsticks should indicate
proper fluid levels.

On a boat with a closed cooling system, there should
be no rust or oily appearance to the coolant in the heat
exchanger's expansion tank. This can be inspected by
removing (on a cold engine) the radiator cap on the tank.

Dirty Bilge Water

Check the bilge. Is the water black and oily? Does it smell
like diesel or gasoline? There should never be any gasoline
or diesel in the bilge unless there's a leaky fuel system.
Gasoline in the bilge can create an explosive situation. A

boat with that condition should not be started until the gasoline is removed legally and the boat well ventilated. Is there an oil-absorbing device in the bilge that is saturated with petro-chemical residue? Bilge water gets dirty only after it comes aboard the boat. Rare is the bilge where a tiny quantity of petroleum has never been accidentally spilled during the routine tasks of changing an oil or fuel filter, but a lot of fuel or oil grime in the bilge indicates a present or previous engine leak.

Drip Pans

The drip pans under the engines should have little or no oil in them. A drop or two that missed the funnel into the valve-cover cap at the last oil change or top-off could run down the block and wind up in the pan. But any large quantity of oil is most likely the result of a bad oil-pan gasket or, worse, leaky crankshaft seals.

Rubber Parts

Marine engines use a fair number of hoses and rubber elbows connecting the piping that distributes cooling water to the heat exchanger, engine oil cooler, etc. Many of these shaped rubber parts are only available from the original engine manufacturer. With some of these specialized two-inch pieces of rubber priced non-competitively for as much as $60 and more apiece, the condition of these rubber parts on an older boat tells a tale about the maintenance attitudes of the previous owner (s). Rubber hoses, belts, and elbows should not be allowed to develop any cracking or flaking before they are replaced. Rubber hoses through which hot water is running always seem to require replacement before their cold-water counterparts.

OIL ANALYSIS AND ENGINE SURVEYS

When what appears to be the right boat is identified and the sale progresses to the point where a surveyor is aboard, it is common to request that the surveyor extract a sample of oil from the engine crankcase and submit it to an oil-analysis lab. Fees for this test can be as low as $20. By having the engine oil scientifically examined and having the types and amounts of various metal and chemical substances measured, a used-boat buyer can be alerted to problems which would not otherwise be discovered without dismantling the engines. The expenses for oil analysis and engine survey are the responsibility of the prospective buyer. When an offer is made, a buyer will want to be sure to state that the offer is "subject to satisfactory hull and mechanical surveys."

12

Drive Lines, Propulsion, and Holes in the Hull

PROP SHAFTS

Most boats larger than trailerable ski boats and day cruisers have inboard engines. Power is transmitted from the gearbox at the aft end of an inboard marine engine to the prop shaft which drives the propeller. As the engine is contained in the hull of the boat and the prop isn't, it becomes necessary to create a hole in the hull for the shaft to pass through. A system of sealing the hole to prevent the introduction of excessive water into the hull is required. The components and condition of this system are important.

Prop shafts can be as simple as a straight, stainless steel shaft from one to three inches in diameter, or as complex as flexible-drive systems with one or more universal joints. Some fairly unique flexible-drive systems have evolved to reduce vibration transmitted up the shaft from the propeller, or to compensate for engines so positioned in the bilge that a straight drive shaft would not produce a desirable angle of relationship between the prop and the hull. A V-drive system often found on boats where engines are mounted just inboard of the transom is an example of a complex drive system. Prop shafts should not be corroded, cracked, or pitted.

Torque Shears and Shaft Brushes

Some drive lines incorporate non-metallic couplers to connect the prop shaft to the output shaft of the transmission. This coupling disc is designed to sacrifice itself if the prop strikes a log or rock, and helps protects against torque damage to the transmission that might result if the controls were accidentally shifted from forward to reverse at high rpm. Non-metallic shaft couplers also assist in isolating the engine from stray low-voltage electrical currents which could travel up the prop shaft and increase corrosion. A thoughtful addition on any boat is the use of a shaft brush, a light piece of narrow copper sheeting or a stainless strap with copper contacts laid across the top of the rotating shaft and connected to the boat's grounding system.

STERN TUBES, CUTLESS BEARINGS, STUFFING BOXES

The prop shaft passes through the hull via an orifice known as a stern tube or shaft log. To allow the shaft to turn in the stern tube, a tiny amount of clearance is required, thus creating an opportunity for water to come aboard the boat.

Cutless Bearings

At the outboard end of the stern tube, the prop shaft is supported by a cutless bearing. Cutless bearings literally require some water to seep between the shaft and the bearing to act as a lubricant when the shaft turns. It is not pos-

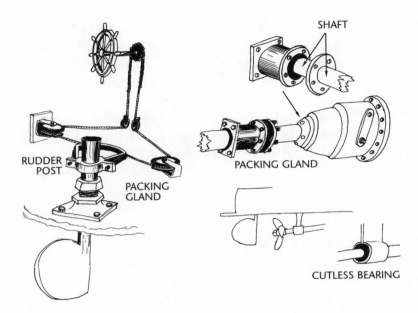

SHAFT

RUDDER POST

PACKING GLAND

PACKING GLAND

CUTLESS BEARING

Some important packing glands and bearings.

sible to inspect the cutless bearing until a boat is hauled out for survey, and at that time the surveyor will check for excessive shaft motion at the bearing.

Stuffing Boxes

At the inboard end of the stern tube, a stuffing box containing flexible packing material (such as Teflon-impregnated flax) prevents most of the water traveling up the shaft from entering the bilge. Like the cutless bearing, the stuffing box is actually water lubricated, and when properly adjusted, a slow dripping occurs from the stuffing box into the bilge. On boats where the prop shaft turns very rapidly, stuffing boxes often have a fitting by which additional water can be injected into the unit to assure adequate lubrication. Excessive dripping can be reduced by tightening the packing nut, causing the materials in the stuffing box to compress more tightly around the shaft. Some boats feature high-tech shaft seals with a bellows-like apparatus and synthetic gasket materials (often lubricated with hydraulic fluids). It is claimed that these shaft seals can actually eliminate water dripping into the bilge from a prop shaft, and like most boating items, these high-tech shaft seals seem to have attracted both devout fans and ardent critics.

Rudder Posts

For each prop shaft there is also a rudder post, a vertical shaft penetrating the hull by which the steering mechanism connects to the rudder blade and controls the rudder angle. Each rudder post has a seal or packing system as well.

INBOARD/OUTBOARD SYSTEMS

Smaller craft often incorporate a drive system known as I/O or inboard/outboard. Unlike a true outboard motor where the steering is controlled by adjusting the horizontal angle of the entire engine assembly relative to the stern of a boat, an I/O configuration allows a usually larger engine to be mounted in a fixed position inboard. Steering is controlled by changing the horizontal angle of adjustable transmission and propeller systems known as outdrives. A large rubber boot seals the rather sizable hole in the stern where the outdrive protrudes, and this boot must be in sound condition for the boat to remain watertight. Outdrives are higher maintenance than a fixed propeller, where the steering is controlled by a rudder. During the survey of any boat with an outdrive, seek an expert opinion on the unit's condition from a marine technician certified by the outdrive manufacturer.

THRU-HULL FITTINGS AND SEACOCKS

Another important consideration below decks is the system of thru-hull fittings and seacocks. In addition to stern tubes, rudder posts, etc., a boat will have several other "holes in the hull," some located below the waterline. Each engine usually has a raw-water intake port through which cooling water is allowed to enter the boat, directed by means of a filter and a hose to the engine. There will be one or more discharge ports for bilge water, one or more inch and a half openings for sewage discharge, and discharge ports for "gray water" from sinks and showers. Rubber hoses connect each of the thru-hull fittings to the engine, bilge pump, or plumbing system as the case may be. As per the theory that a chain is no stronger than its weakest link, even the stoutest hull afloat depends on the integrity of the rubber hoses connected to thru-hull fittings to keep water from entering the hull at a disastrous rate. As rubber hoses may break or leak and require occasional replacement, a valve known as a seacock will be

A thru-hull seacock with double clamped hose.

fitted to each thru-hull to close the intake or discharge port in the event of an emergency or when changing a hose.

Seacock Maintenance

Hoses connected to seacocks should be double clamped at both ends for an extra margin of safety. Some seacocks are made of plastic materials (and there are undoubtedly some who might claim advantages for the plastic above and beyond lowest possible cost). But the closer any boat approaches to becoming a "yacht," the more likely the thru-hull fittings and seacocks will be bronze. Prudent boaters lubricate all of the seacocks twice a year and test them for proper operation. On a used boat you might see round, tapered, wooden plugs fastened by a line to each thru-hull, indicating the previous owner has prepared dealing with the emergency of a hose failure combined with a seacock stuck in the open position. When inspecting a boat under serious consideration, ask the owner or broker to operate a few of the seacocks to evaluate whether they are working properly. Frozen seacocks can often be dismantled, cleaned, lubricated, and returned to service, but for seacocks at or below the waterline this can only be done with the boat hauled out.

A boater was once heard to remark that he didn't bother to service his thru-hull fittings since most of them were above the waterline. A second boater replied, "How long would they be above the waterline if you began to sink?" The first boater spent the rest of the afternoon freeing up and greasing the seacocks.

13

Bilge Pumps

NUMBER OF PUMPS

While in the engine room area, use this opportunity to inspect for adequate bilge pumps. As with most systems on a boat, redundancy is *very* desirable in bilge pumps. One electric and one manual pump are a bare minimum. Either pump should be able to remove water at a rate sufficient to maintain flotation in all but the most disastrous circumstances. A second 12-volt pump is not extravagant, and for boats which will spend most of the time at the dock connected to shore power (possibly without inspection for up to several days at a time), a high-capacity AC pump will assist in keeping a boat afloat in the event that the 12-volt pumps burn out or the batteries become exhausted. In the event of serious flooding underway, the boat's engines can actually assist in pumping the bilges if a boater closes the seacocks for raw cooling-water intake, disconnects the intake hose from the thru-hull, and draws the engine cooling water from the bilge instead. No boat should rely on a single bilge pump. Bilge pumps on most pleasure craft are too few and of too-small a capacity to adequately evacuate bilge water in the event of a serious hull breach. But they can assist in remaining afloat while emergency repairs are made—i.e., a seacock closed or a piece of canvas or plastic secured across the out-side of a ruptured hull)—or at the very least slow the rate of sinkage, buying time for rescue or evacuation.

BILGE PUMP CAPACITIES

The failure of a hose attached to a one-inch thru-hull fitting a couple of feet below the waterline will bring water aboard a vessel at about 28 gallons a minute (1,680 gallons/hour). The rated capacity of any bilge pump is subject to reduc-tion if you have to pump water either higher or farther than the standard under which the pump has been tested. So a bilge pump rated at anything less than 2,000 gallons per hour will have a difficult time keeping the boat afloat. A small boat does not call for a small bilge pump; in fact the reverse is true. While a medium-sized boat might remain afloat with a few thousand pounds of water in the bilge, a small runabout or day cruiser would often have settled to the bottom with far less. It is even more critical that the small boat's bilge pump keep pace with incoming water. Water comes aboard through a given-sized hull breach very democratically, with absolutely no handicap awarded to various sizes of boats.

Discharge Ports

Well-plumbed bilge pumps will pump bilge water overboard above the waterline. Some boats are designed with dis-charge ports for bilge water at or below the waterline, in which case there must be a loop in the discharge line to pre-vent water from entering the bilge through the very hose intended to remove it. The loop and longer hose length reduce significantly a bilge pump's efficiency in the gallons per hour claimed by the manufacturer.

Switches

A well-designed system will have both manual and automatic switches for each electric pump. The automatic or float switches are placed in the bottom of the bilge and activate a pump when the water level reaches a predetermined depth (usually about two and a half or three inches) and shut it off when the water drops to a level of less than an inch or so. The simplest of these switches feature a hinged, hollow plastic arm which floats into a horizontal position as bilge water accumulates. These switches contain a large globule of mercury which flows back and forth as the arm's angle changes and through which electrical contact is made. (A point to note in the event that a float switch ever becomes physically broken and must be handled: *mercury is dangerously toxic*). The more deluxe float switches often incorporate such features as a sensor to shut off the pump if oil is being pumped overboard, and guards or screens to protect the float from becoming jammed in the "on" position by a bit of stray debris floating in the bilge.

Manual switches allow a boater to turn on a bilge pump in spite of a malfunctioning float switch or to drain the bilge more completely than an automatic switch might. In days of greater environmental apathy it was common for boaters to routinely pump the entire contents of their bilge overboard at frequent intervals (often waste-water holding tanks as well), and the manual switch was used for this purpose. More enlightened boaters today confine the pumping of the bilge while underway to the frequency dictated by the float switches and will await an opportunity at a sewage pump-out facility to suck the bilge completely dry.

Fortunately, most pleasure boaters will never face a situation where the bilge pumps are all that maintains flotation, *but every boater must be mentally prepared and adequately equipped for just such an event.*

14

Fuel Systems

IF THE ENGINE IS THE HEART of a powerboat, the fuel is the blood. While in the engine room (aren't you glad you came down here?), you usually have the best opportunity to visually evaluate the fuel system of a boat.

FUEL TANKS

Because of the weight of fuel (350 gallons weighs well over a ton), the location of fuel tanks on a vessel is an important element of initial design. Commonly, fuel is stored in equal quantities and drawn simultaneously from separate port and starboard tanks, or in some smaller boats from a single tank centered in the bilge area.

Fuel tanks typically are made of aluminum, but on many older boats they are constructed of black iron. Iron fuel tanks present the risk of failure through corrosion. Older aluminum tanks will fail on rare occasions as well, typically as the result of inadequate welding or the use of an improper alloy by the manufacturer. When a fuel tank fails aboard a boat, the loss of a few hundred dollars worth of fuel will be the least of a skipper's worries. Any fuel leaked into the bilge may be pumped overboard by the bilge pump (in the absence of smart switches which will shut the pump off when high concentrations of gas or oil are detected in the bilge water). *Any oil pumped overboard must, by law, be reported to the Coast Guard.* The discharged fuel becomes the boater's responsibility to contain and clean up, and failure to adequately clean up spilled fuel or oil can result in a fine of up to $20,000. While the cost of purchasing a replacement tank may be hundreds of dollars, the cost of dismantling and reassembling enough of the boat to allow the new tank to be installed will frequently be thousands.

Plastic Fuel Tanks

On some newer boats, plastic fuel tanks are becoming common. Some experts opine that plastic tanks are superior to aluminum because there is no opportunity for the welds to fail or for any metal disintegration whatsoever. Plastic has no tendency to rust or corrode, is lighter in weight and less costly to produce. Plastic tanks can be custom molded to fit into many of the irregularly shaped spaces on a boat and could conceivably allow more elbow space in the engine room. Someday we may all be boating with plastic fuel tanks, but then again we may not.

VENTS, VALVES, AND DECK FITTINGS

All fuel tanks must be vented so that air can escape as it is displaced by incoming fuel. A metal fuel tank must be grounded. Tanks should have valves at the point where the fuel supply line to the engine connects so that fuel can be shut off in the event of downstream leakage or when servicing fuel filters. Fuel will normally be pumped aboard through a separate deck fitting for each fuel tank. When back on deck, it will be interesting to note whether the deck fittings are labeled or not. Sometimes deck fittings for totally different systems are located side by side and the lack of a label cast into the base of the fitting can be confusing. A veteran boater of my acquaintance once pumped a hundred gallons of gasoline into the freshwater tank of his boat early one foggy morning through an unlabeled freshwater deck fitting located inches away from the also unlabeled fuel deck fitting. Some labels are on the threaded cap of the fitting itself. In such a case it is very helpful if the deck fittings are of differing diameters to prevent the accidental replacement of a labeled cap into an improper opening!

FUEL CAPACITY AND RANGE

Fuel capacity will help determine the adaptability of a boat for certain types of cruising. Boaters who venture into remote areas may find it necessary to plan a cruise from fuel dock to fuel dock—where they will have to pay whatever price is being asked—if they burn dozens of gallons of fuel per hour and only have a few hundred gallons of capacity. Some boaters can cruise all season on 300 gallons, while others will use that much in a three-day weekend. For boaters planning extended offshore cruises the range of a vessel becomes important.

Range is calculated by dividing fuel capacity by gallons per hour consumed times cruising speed. A boat which travels at 12 knots while burning 9 gallons of fuel per hour would have a range of 396 nautical miles if she carries 300 gallons of fuel. A boat which cruises at 25 knots while burning 40 gallons per hour would need 600 gallons of fuel capacity to achieve a range of 375 nautical miles, while an 8-knot vessel with 300 gallons of fuel burning at 2½ gallons per hour has a range of almost 1,000 nautical miles. A practical skipper will try to refuel before exhausting more than three quarters of the fuel supply, so the effective practical range of a boat is actually only about 75 percent of the theoretical range established by the fuel capacity.

FUEL AGING AND STABILITY

Too much fuel aboard can have drawbacks as well, making a boat unnecessarily heavy and allowing the fuel to become so old that it destabilizes. Gasoline allowed to sit for an extended period will lose some of its more volatile components through evaporation, resulting in greater difficulty when starting a cold engine. Diesel fuel in particular can become a little quirky when allowed to age for too long, from both destabilization of the original fuel chemistry as well as a tendency to foster the growth of a filter-clogging "fuel fungus." Various miracle goops and additives are sold to prevent destabilization of fuels and to kill off diesel scum bugs, but keeping a fresh rotation of fuel through the tanks is the recommended method of prevention. Keeping fuel tanks fairly full will reduce the amount of water forming from condensation on the inside of a partially emptied tank, so the temptation to purchase less than a tankful should be avoided, even at the risk of possibly having to deal with an overaged fuel supply.

Conscientious boaters try to purchase fuel from established, high-volume suppliers whenever possible to help assure a fresh and fairly contamination-free fill-up. Many boaters who must fuel up outside of the U.S. or Canada carry Baja filters, large funnel-like devices placed at the fuel intake port while filling up, and intended to trap much of the water, rust, and dirt which often contaminates fuel in less-developed countries.

WATER SEPARATION AND FUEL FILTERING

The old cliché states that "oil and water do not mix," but they will certainly make one heck of an effort to do so in the fuel systems of most boats. Some water may be pumped into the fuel tanks at the fuel dock, and some may form as a result of condensation. Warm fuel being pumped back into a cool fuel tank from the return line of a diesel injection pump will accelerate condensation. As water accumulates it settles to the bottom of the fuel tank and is drawn off through the fuel line. Between the fuel tank and the engine on most boats is a filtering system which incorporates a water-separation feature. Water accumulates in a bowl below the fuel filter. Frequently this bowl is transparent so that by means of visual inspection it is possible to tell when enough water has accumulated that the bowl must be drained off.

By checking the appearance of the collecting bowl on fuel/water separators, a prospective purchaser can determine whether there is a lot of water being removed from the fuel system or at least how recently the bowl may have been emptied. Water will appear clear, while gasoline is typically slightly yellow looking, and diesel fuel is commonly dyed red. Some boaters prefer trying to flush the water through the engine rather than filtering it out and will use fuel-drying additives. Most of these additives rely on alcohol to emulsify any water trapped in a fuel system, and alcohol is a chemical that most experts recommend against introducing into an engine.

Primary and Secondary Filters

Fuel should be filtered through both primary and secondary filters, with the secondary or final filter often mounted on the engine itself. Initial filtering can be as coarse as 30 microns ($\frac{30}{100}$ of a millimeter) allowing emulsified water and foreign particles smaller than this to pass through, although 10 microns is more common. Secondary filters are frequently as fine as 2 microns. All engines require clean fuel, but diesel boaters must be particularly conscious of having an adequate fuel-filtering system and maintaining it regularly. How easy will it be to service the filters on the boat under consideration? If filter changing appears to be a serious problem (perhaps the engine was configured with the secondary filter buried behind a lot of plumbing), there may have been an inadequate number of filter changes in the past.

FUEL LINES

Copper tubing is the material of choice for fuel lines. Copper resists corrosion and can be shaped to fit the available space between fuel tanks and primary filters. The flexibility of copper allows it to avoid becoming brittle and cracking due to continual engine vibrations. It should be possible to follow the run of a fuel line by eye from the tank to the primary and secondary filters, and there should be no leaks at any of the joints. A well-designed fuel line does not contain splices in the middle of a run.

15

Cooling and Exhaust Systems

MOST PEOPLE ARE FAMILIAR with the cooling of automobile engines through a radiator which transfers heat removed from the engine into the air. Air radiation requires an enormous amount of air to pass across the cooling fins. While a sufficient amount of air can pour through the grille of an automobile, no such phenomenon exists in the engine room of a boat. Provisions must be made to remove the heat in another manner, and a boat has the advantage of operating while immersed in a fabulous heat-absorbing medium: water.

CLOSED COOLING SYSTEMS

Marine engines with closed cooling systems are cooled by constantly pumping water aboard the boat, where it is circulated around a series of tubes known as the heat exchanger. A permanent engine coolant or antifreeze circulates through the engine block and heads, and flows through the heat exchanger's tubes. The heat exchanger performs much the same function as an automobile radiator, transferring heat collected by the engine coolant to the much lower-temperature raw water introduced from outside of the hull. The raw water will also circulate through any oil coolers or turbo aftercoolers installed on the engine. Oil coolers use a heat exchanger to reduce the temperature of engine oil and will assist in maintaining adequate oil pressure and proper lubrication qualities. Turbo aftercoolers refrigerate air after it is compressed by the turbo charger, increasing its density so that more oxygen molecules are contained in a given cubic volume, enhancing the combustion process in the engine. Most higher-horsepower diesels are turbo charged, but no gasoline engines for marine applications would ever utilize a turbo.

RAW-WATER COOLING

Raw-water cooling systems pump fresh- or saltwater from outside the hull directly through the entire engine cooling system, including the block and heads, without a heat exchanger or an antifreeze coolant. Engines subjected to higher operating temperatures may be more efficiently cooled with a raw-water approach.

MANIFOLD COOLING AND MUFFLING

After circulating through the various heat exchangers found in the engine and through water jackets built into the exhaust manifold (nobody wants a red-hot exhaust manifold in an engine room), the cooling water is pumped back overboard through the exhaust system. Water flowing through the exhaust pipes acts as a muffler to quiet the exhaust and keeps the exhaust tubing from becoming overly hot as well. To make sure that the cooling system is working, boaters develop the habit, each time the engine is started, of watching for the splash of cooling water discharged from the exhaust system.

RAW-WATER STRAINERS

Each engine should be equipped with a raw-water intake strainer to remove seaweed and other debris from the cooling water before it is circulated through the engine. Often these filters are contained in a transparent housing. When inspecting a boat for potential purchase, note the condition of the strainers and whether or not they appear to have been kept clean. A vessel on the market with a green salad in the raw-water strainer may have been operated in a condition where the engine was not adequately cooled, an indication that the previous owner did not pay enough attention to maintenance.

WATER PUMPS

A marine engine with a closed cooling system has two pumps that require occasional service to insure that an engine will cool properly. The first is the raw-water pump which circulates water brought aboard for cooling purposes and then pumps it out again. The raw-water pump is the only cooling pump found on a boat with a raw-water cooling system. This pump is ordinarily gear driven, and contains a rubber impeller that is subject to eventual wear, requiring occasional replacement. If a maintenance log has been kept on a used boat, see how recently the raw-water impeller was changed. Some experts recommend changing this impeller annually. Others favor "leaving well enough alone," unless some indication—such as a reduced flow of cooling water from the exhaust pipe or a higher-than-normal reading on the temperature gauge—creates grounds to suspect a deteriorating component.

The second pump is the usually belt-driven engine coolant or water pump which circulates the freshwater and antifreeze mix through the block and heads, absorbing the heat transferred to the raw water at the heat exchanger. The water pump on a marine engine is similar in design and application to that found on the family car. Boaters who venture far offshore will usually have a spare water pump aboard and be confident that somebody aboard has the knowledge to install it if the need arises. When overhauling a gasoline engine, or after about 2,000–3000 hours on a diesel (check the manufacturer's recommendations), it's a good idea to replace a water pump as a preventive measure.

EXHAUST SYSTEMS

Exhaust manifolds and heat exchangers will have sacrificial zinc anodes. These zincs must be replaced regularly, often three times a year or more, to prevent corrosion of critical internal components and manifold baffling. Exhaust manifold corrosion can, in some cases, lead to complete engine failure. Boats listed for sale often advertise "new exhaust manifold," as the manifold is the component most often requiring replacement due to exposure to heat and corrosive elements. The presence of a few spare zincs in the engine room may indicate that the previous owner took this task seriously. Zincs should be changed frequently enough so that the zinc material on the end of the installation nut will remain in adequate quantity and condition to be effective. In most cases, this will be of sufficient frequency that the brass nut on the end remains clean and bright looking. A zinc nut which has been painted over might be cause for major concern.

Exhaust Elbows and Hose

An engine installed below the waterline will direct exhaust gases upward to a point above the waterline, then through an exhaust elbow and back down to bilge level, to eventually exit just above the waterline at the stern. The elbow above the waterline helps prevent a following sea from rushing up the exhaust pipe and entering the engine. A well-designed exhaust system incorporates some type of support to bear the weight of the exhaust elbow and relieve strain on the manifold. Connections between the elbow and the exhaust hose should be tight, and there should be no sooty-looking patches on the underside of the deck above the exhaust system. Carbon monoxide can enter a boat through a compromised exhaust hose, so it's an excellent idea to see that the hose runs unrestricted to the stern and has not developed any rusty or sooty patches along its length.

Dry Stack Exhaust

Most commercial vessels and a few pleasure boats use a dry-stack exhaust system in which the exhaust gases exit through a vertical exhaust pipe terminating well above the cabintop level. The disadvantage of a dry stack is that the exhaust cloud then tends to settle over any boat which might be moving slowly on a calm day.

16

Electrical Systems

IF THE ENGINE IS THE HEART of a powerboat and the fuel is the blood, the 12-volt batteries must roughly correspond to an important part of the central nervous system. Without adequate 12-volt power to crank and start an engine, a powerboat is totally disabled. While below decks on a powerboat under consideration for purchase, spend some time evaluating the adequacy, convenience, and condition of the battery system.

THE BATTERY SYSTEM

Battery Types

Marine batteries have historically been of the wet-cell variety, which requires the occasional topping off with distilled water. When you look into a battery cell, it becomes quickly evident whether the battery has been sufficiently maintained. Batteries in which the electrolyte has been allowed to dissipate to the point where the plates have become partially dry are candidates for replacement in the near future. Many neglected wet-cell marine batteries are allowed to be maintenance free in practice, in spite of the fact that the battery manufacturers never intended them as such. Some

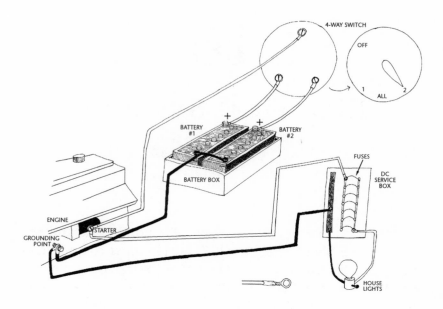

A simple 12-volt electrical system.

of the more costly marine batteries today are of the gel-cell variety, completely sealed units with a gelled electrolyte instead of a liquid. Gel-celled batteries could theoretically be installed sideways or upside down without danger of leakage, and some battery companies claim that their gel cells can be discharged to zero capacity and then recharged with virtually no loss of electrical potential.

A prospective purchaser should note the type of batteries installed on a vessel, and their relative ages. Most batteries will have a date-of-sale tag attached for warranty purposes. It is good boating practice to replace entire groups of batteries at a time as having batteries of various ages connected to the same charging system can result in some peculiar recharging irregularities. Gel-cell and wet-cell batteries should never be mixed on a boat as they accept current quite differently when recharging from the alternator or the 110-volt A/C battery charger.

Battery Isolation

Any powerboat large enough to have electrically operated accessories should have a minimum of two batteries, with one engine battery reserved strictly for providing power to crank the engine. The 12-volt lights, refrigeration, stereo systems, navigation electronics, etc. then operate from the second, or house battery. These two batteries are isolated from one another by a battery-selector switch which allows a boater to access either the house or engine battery independently (or both at once to facilitate recharging from the engine's alternator while underway). This switch is sometimes located in the bilge area near the batteries—probably to reduce the amount of time and wire needed to install it—but it is far more convenient if it is located near a helm station. If the selector switch is in the engine room, it will be necessary for the skipper to visit the engine room after starting the boat on the engine battery to rotate the switch to the "all" or "both" position while underway and to enter the engine room again upon reaching the destination to switch the selector to the "house" position.

Battery-selector switches also have an "off" position to disconnect the batteries from the boat's electrical system. Care must be taken that the "off" position is never selected while an engine is running, as severe alternator damage (blown diodes) will most likely result.

Battery Banks

Many boats have more than two batteries. Twin-engine boats often have a starting battery for each engine, and boaters who anchor out for extended periods of time without a generator or access to shore power will frequently use a bank of house batteries. A battery bank is created when batteries are connected in such a manner that the positive and negative terminals are wired to the identical terminals on the other batteries in the bank. Connecting the opposite terminals (positive to negative) of two 12-volt batteries creates a 24-volt system which would fry the electrical system of most pleasure craft.

Battery Boxes

Batteries onboard should be contained in battery boxes. A battery box captures any spilled electrolyte, and the cover of the box protects the terminals from coming into accidental contact with a wrench or other metal object, which could conceivably result in a dangerous or damaging electrical short circuit. Battery boxes must be secured by bolts, screws, or straps to prevent batteries from shifting and sliding around the bilge as a boat pitches and rolls in heavy seas.

Battery Capacity

A fair-sized powerboat can easily use 150 or more amp hours of 12-volt power a day, and to maximize battery life it is important not to draw most wet-cell batteries down below 50 percent of rated capacity. A 150-amp-hour-per-day boat (without an onboard generator) anchored out for three days requires a house battery bank of two 450-amp batteries or three 300-amp batteries to avoid discharging beyond the 50 percent level, or the engine needs to be operated at regular intervals to restore battery power. When considering a powerboat, determine whether it has adequate battery capacity for your anticipated usage and, if not, whether there is room available to add additional batteries.

DISTRIBUTION PANELS

With the possible exception of a high-water alarm or a bilge pump, no accessories should be wired directly to the house battery, and nothing should draw from the engine battery except the engine's starting motor. Wiring circuits for accessories should all terminate at a distribution panel from which either AC or DC current can be switched on or off with circuit breakers. On any boat, but particularly an older boat lacking many of the modern electronic navigation devices, see whether any additional breakers can be added to the panel. If a panel has no room for additional breakers, circuits can sometimes be made available by eliminating obsolete equipment, i.e., a radio direction finder circuit could be used to power a modern GPS chartplotter. (Such changes may have already been made by the previous owner of a used vessel, with or without the benefit of properly relabeling the breakers.) Another option on a boat without adequate electrical capacity at the distribution panel is to install an additional panel elsewhere on the boat. Most distribution panels will incorporate AC and/or DC amp or volt meters to assist the boater in monitoring electrical system conditions.

WIRE

One area in which a boat builder's dedication to quality and craftsmanship is visually apparent is in the type of wiring used and how it is organized. Wire should be of marine grade, typically a high-quality stranded (not solid) wire, to better withstand vibration without breaking. Hot wires, negative wires, and ground wires should all follow a consistent color scheme for easy identification. Well-built boats always have wires arranged on wire looms or conduits, wrapped in bundles and well secured. Lack of basic wire organization could indicate a hurry-up attitude in a vessel's construction or subsequent modification. The wires behind the service panel should not look like a rat's nest. Wire nuts so commonly used in household wiring have no place in the marine environment, where wire connections should be crimped or swaged with proper fittings and sealed against moisture. Heat-shrink tubing is becoming commonplace for sealing electrical connections. Although electrician's tape can be used for sealing a properly fastened connection, it should never be used to wrap two wires that are just simply twisted together.

INVERTERS AND GENERATORS

While most electrical items on board are operable in 12-volt DC mode, occasions arise when it is desirable to operate power tools, microwave ovens, or other 120-volt AC electrical items when not connected to shore power. An inverter or motorized generator can be used, depending on the space available and the amount of power required.

Inverters

An inverter is like a battery charger operating in reverse. Instead of using AC power to make DC current for purposes of charging a battery, an inverter discharges a battery by withdrawing DC amperage and changing it to 110/120-volt AC current. An inverter takes up very little space and can be accommodated on practically any sized boat. Since inverters are solid-state electronic devices, they operate quietly and unobtrusively. Inverters are primarily suitable for intermittent or occasional AC usage, such as running a TV/VCR for a few hours in the evening or plugging in a pot to brew breakfast coffee. Inverters will ultimately draw the house battery down to the point where it will need to be recharged by an onboard generator, running the main engines to activate the alternators, or connecting to shore power and allowing the onboard battery charger to restore potential amperage. Most inverters incorporate a system to shut the inversion process down when the battery level becomes critically low.

Generators

For high electrical loads such as electric space heaters, hot-water tanks, and all-electric galleys (as well as for boats which will be anchored out a lot), a gasoline or diesel generator makes a lot of sense. Boats with all-electric galleys need a system which will supply 110-volt power to refrigerators and stoves while underway. A high-output alternator driven as an accessory by the main engine or a separate AC generator may be used to create large amounts of 110-volt current. Some boats incorporate very small one-cylinder diesel engines, consuming about a quart of diesel per hour, dedicated to the sole task of running a DC generator and creating a source with which to recharge the battery banks.

Generators do occupy precious space on a boat and add to the costs of acquisition and maintenance, which may explain why generators are almost never found on boats less than 32 feet. At 38–40 feet and above, it is fairly rare for a boat not to be equipped with a generator. Generators are available in either gas or diesel versions and can draw fuel from the main fuel supply. A gasoline generator in an enclosed space will need to have a blower fan operating fairly constantly when the vessel is not underway or has slowed to the point where the normal air flow through the engine room may not be sufficient to expel fuel vapors. A well-installed generator is properly grounded, properly vented and exhausted, well mounted (not too close to the main stateroom if possible), and contained within a sound shield to control noise. Noise is the number one generator-related complaint. Many boaters have bitter memories of nights spent in what should be pristine wilderness anchorages listening to the chugging exhaust of a neighboring boater's generator. Some generators installed in engine rooms can be rigged to provide "get home" power to a prop shaft and allow a vessel to limp in, should the main engine fail.

ELECTROLYSIS AND CORROSION

Whenever two diverse metals are connected by a conductive medium such as water or battery acid, the more noble metal will extract electrons from the less noble metal, and corrosion will occur. Corrosion on a boat is controlled by the use of ground wires and sacrificial zinc anodes. Zinc is one of the least noble of metals, and by attaching zinc fittings to prop shafts, rudders, trim tabs, etc., the electrical charges which must absorb electrons from other metals obtain these electrons from the zinc rather than from the critical and incredibly expensive structural components of the vessel.

Grounding

Electrical systems on boats are grounded to the water surrounding the hull (except when operating on shore power). Metal fittings which contact water, such as bronze seacocks, should have a ground wire running from each fitting to a grounding strap. This ground wire will absorb stray electrical currents which accelerate corrosion. Bronze fittings which are turning green and covered with a crumbling, powderlike residue are not properly grounded and may need to be replaced if the corrosion process cannot be arrested in time. As previously noted, grounding the prop shaft is an excellent idea, accomplished by placing a flat, metal shaft brush where it will ride across the top of the shaft as it turns, and connecting the brush to the grounding system.

17

When Nature Calls

WHILE STILL BELOW DECKS, the opportunity is ripe (hopefully not too ripe!) to evaluate the boat's sewage system. Not so many years ago the sewage system on a boat was a pretty simple affair: one simply flushed the head by pumping the contents overboard. Out of sight, out of mind. In our more enlightened modern times, the cleanliness of our waterways has become increasingly emphasized, and there is no group who will benefit more from cleaner, less-contaminated water than recreational boaters. Soapy water from sinks and showers may still be drained directly overboard in most localities. Water containing solid or liquid human waste cannot be pumped out without proper sterilization treatment, unless a vessel is more than three miles from shore, and then only in the open ocean. (Dumping sewage overboard three and a half miles from shore in a seven-mile-wide bay or estuary will leave a boater liable for fines which could exceed the purchase price of a modest boat.)

TYPE I AND TYPE III SANITATION SYSTEMS

There are two approaches to the sewage problem: sewage is either treated in a Coast Guard-approved sterilization device and then pumped overboard or is stored aboard the boat in a holding tank which will eventually be emptied at a designated pump-out facility connected to a shoreside sewage treatment system. Most boats with a certified treatment system will still utilize a holding tank to contain treated waste awaiting pump out, for those occasions when a boater is anchored in a crowded harbor and would just as soon not send the contents of the head (not withstanding proper disinfection) floating past the other boats anchored there. The certified treat-and-release systems are known as Type I systems, while the holding-tank-only approach is known as a Type III. Technically speaking, waste treated in a Type I system and then stored in Type III holding tank becomes Type III material and should be disposed at a dockside pump out, since bacteria can re-form as the waste is held in the tank.

Type I

Two commonly available Type I methods are the acid bath and the boiler. An acid-bath system uses the salt in seawater (or salt from a salt tank when operating in freshwater) and electrical current to create hypochlorous acid. The sewage is then soaked in the acid for a few minutes until all traces of fecal coliform bacteria have been eliminated and is then directed either overboard or into a holding tank for more discreet disposal at a later time. The boiler systems don't actually boil the sewage, but they do raise the temperature of the stuff to a point where the bacteria cannot survive. Both systems use a large amount of 12-volt amperage when operating, and it can be advisable to run an engine or generator while processing waste to ease the load on the batteries.

Type III Systems and Y valves

Type III systems usually incorporate a Y valve, which directs sewage either directly overboard where legal or into

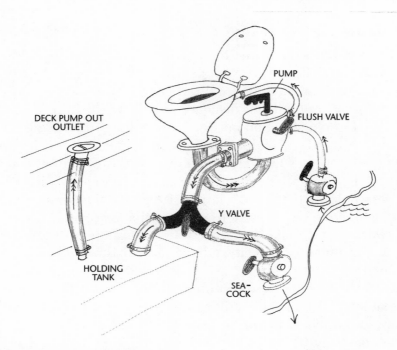

Typical marine toilet system.

the holding tank. The position of the Y valve is one of the items often examined when a boat operating less than three miles offshore is boarded by the Coast Guard for a routine inspection. The Coast Guard will expect the valve to be wired or zip-tied into a position whereby waste can only flow to the holding tank. When full, Type III systems are emptied at pump-out facilities which are becoming common at fuel docks and marinas. A deck fitting with a hose connected to the holding tank will facilitate pump out and eliminate the fairly unpleasant task of dragging the pump-out suction hose down into the bilge and manually opening an access port on the tank itself. On an extended offshore voyage in unrestricted waters, a Type III system may be legally emptied by onboard pumps moving the sewage directly overboard. The two most common pumps are the electric macerator style or a manual diaphragm-type unit.

Holding-Tank Capacity

In general, boaters must be aware that the laws regarding sewage discharge from vessels are likely to become even stricter with time. Some localities currently and soon many more may prohibit the discharge of all waste from a boat without any distinction between treated and untreated. An adequately sized holding tank is an important consideration. A family of four anchored out for the weekend, each using the head a half-dozen times a day can easily fill a 25-gallon holding tank, and a larger size is called for if cruising plans include being away from a marina for several days at a time. It can make sense to draw a parallel between the cruising range of a boat and the size of the holding tank which would be appropriate. Most boaters pump out at fuel docks. A high-speed, short-range boat can justify a somewhat smaller tank (unless long, camped-out anchorages are a predominant cruising pattern) by virtue of the fact that the boat may be fueling up near a pump out station every couple of days or so anyway.

Many new boats are equipped with truly inadequate holding tanks as the manufacturers are concerned with meeting the letter of the law at the cheapest possible cost. On a boat any larger than a simple runabout (where portable toilets are usually found rather than any permanent sanitation plumbing), a 10-flush holding tank about the size of a breadbox may simply be one of the more visible indicators of a boat built to a budget instead of a standard. There are new boats on the market where the holding tank isn't even properly fastened down!

SANITATION HOSES

The type and condition of the hoses which connect the head to the treatment device or the holding tank as well as the hose from the holding tank to the discharge ports on deck and at the thru-hull should be examined. The best available hose is a heavy black hose clearly labeled for use in a sanitation system. This hose can be a little difficult to bend and costs several dollars a foot more than other available sewer hoses. Many of the other hoses in use are similar to a vacuum-system hose, but need to be made out of waste-resistant materials, as the chemicals found in human waste tend to break down many varieties of plastic and rubber fairly quickly. The cheaper hoses require replacement every few years to control both leakage and the escape of odoriferous gas. The better grade of hose doesn't last indefinitely either, but will probably be the less expensive hose overall on a per-year-of-service basis in spite of a much higher initial cost. On a used boat, look carefully at the apparent age of the hoses as well as for signs of cracking or brittleness and for the presence of any suspicious-looking stains beneath hose connections or under the low point of any dip or loop in the hose. There should be no discernible sewage smell on a properly operating and maintained system.

HIGH-TECH MARINE TOILETS

On some boats there may be a large vacuum tank incorporated into the plumbing for the head(s) as part of a vacuum-flushing system. Such systems take up some space and will add to the cost of a boat, but they offer the advantage of low-water-volume flushes which can increase the number of days a less-than-generously sized holding tank will function without requiring a trip to the pump-out station. Marine heads which flush by push-button are popular as well, and many of these macerate, or grind up, any solids as they evacuate the bowl.

GRAY WATER AND SUMPS

Gray water draining from sinks and showers will drain overboard, by gravity, where the sink or shower drain is above the waterline. Shower drains particularly are very often below the waterline, and water will drain into a small, few-gallon-capacity sump from which it will have to be discharged by a designated pump. A boat with a well-designed shower sump will leave little or no standing water in the sump when the pump cycle has finished. Odors from soapy shower water left to cook in a warm engine room can waft back up through the shower drain and into the formal berthing spaces.

18

Freshwater Supply

"WATER, WATER EVERYWHERE but not a drop to drink..." or shower with, shave, do dishes, make soup, cook shellfish, make coffee, or wipe down the refrigerator, unless there's adequate freshwater aboard and it's conveniently available where and when needed.

TANK CAPACITY AND LOCATION

The location of the freshwater storage tank is important in the design of a boat, since at eight pounds per gallon, 150–300 gallons adds up pretty quickly. Since the weight of the tank's contents drops as the water is consumed, it isn't practical to simply balance a large tank by placing it opposite, say, four 8D batteries and a generator. The lower in the bilge and the more central the location of the tank, the better. Because of the need to locate a water tank low in the bilge, water will need to be pumped to any location where it is desired for use. Some boats have two water tanks directly abeam of one another and draw water from them simultaneously. The size of tank needed on a boat is determined in part by the vessel's cruising patterns. A boat anchored out for a week with a family of five aboard would require a 300-gallon capacity to supply 8.5 gallons per person per day. A couple who cruises strictly from city marina to city marina could get by with far less.

Venting and Grounding

A freshwater tank needs to be vented so that, as the water level in the tank rises and falls, air can be inducted or displaced as necessary and no vacuum or pressurization allowed to build up in the tank. Ideally, the vent should be well above the waterline (or a loop will need to be placed in the line) to prevent possible contamination of the freshwater supply by seawater finding its way into the vent through wave action or a thoughtless nearby boater's excessive wake. A metal water tank will also need to be connected to the vessel's grounding system. A drain valve on a water tank is a handy feature to empty the tank for winterization or drain water which may have become contaminated and allow the tank to be cleaned.

PRESSURE PUMPS

Water pressure is achieved by a 12-volt pump. Some systems also incorporate pressure-regulation tanks which maintain steady water pressure to open faucets without the typical fast-hammer cycling experienced on water systems without a regulator tank. Once activated by a manual switch, a pump will run as required to maintain a pre-set water pressure in the lines on the pressurized side of the pump.

HOT-WATER TANKS

The 12-volt pump directs water to both the cold-water faucets and to the hot-water tank. A marine hot-water tank heats water by 110-volt electrical elements when connected to shore power or a generator, or by extracting heat from the engine coolant (which is piped through a heat exchanger inside the tank). As small tanks recover heat fairly quickly, the hot-water tank on most boats does not need to be much over a 10- or 20-gallon capacity. Some larger boats with 50- to 80-gallon soaking tubs in the head will need a proportionately larger hot-water tank (as well as jumbo-capacity freshwater storage). The output side of the hot-water tank supplies all of the hot-water faucets aboard. Noting the accessibility of the hot-water tank will give a boater an idea of just how large a chore it will be when the tank inevitably requires removal and replacement.

FRESHWATER MAKERS

Boats intended for extended offshore cruising will typically use a water purifying system to filter or distill seawater, insuring an endless supply of freshwater (as long as the system is working). A water-making system is another case where redundancy is desirable. A permanently installed system could be backed up by a hand-operated liferaft-type device, or enough spare parts and technical knowledge to rebuild the system while at sea.

DOCKSIDE HOSE CONNECTIONS
AND WATER LINES

Boaters who spend large amounts of time docked at marinas appreciate a freshwater inlet which allows the boat to connect (through a water hose) to the municipal water supply. Hose bib-type freshwater inlets have a pressure regulator to prevent excess water pressure dockside from bursting freshwater hoses or otherwise damaging the plumbing. Water lines throughout the vessel may be either copper or plastic and should be leakfree at all connections.

SOME THINGS TO LOOK FOR

On a used boat, signs of present or previous leakage, such as stains under plumbing connections or warped cabinet bottoms under galley or head sinks, can alert a prospective owner to areas which, if not in need of urgent repair, may well be worth closely observing in the future. Many boats use freshwater pumps which switch on automatically as water pressure downstream from the pump drops, such as when a faucet is opened and water is drawn off. If all of the faucets are completely closed, this pump will not switch on unless there is a water leak on the pressurized side of the pump. If, during the inspection process, the freshwater pump circuit breaker is on and a water pump is heard cycling in occasional two- or three-second intervals there is either a dripping faucet or a leak from a hose or connection. Neither a plumbing leak nor a dripping faucet is acceptable on a vessel with a finite freshwater supply and will need to be corrected. While boats are designed to be used in water, it is truly amazing the amount of time that boaters spend keeping water contained where desired aboard and out of places where they would rather the water not be!

19

Heat, Ventilation, and Air Conditioning

T HERE ARE CERTAINLY MANY components of a boat far more glamorous than its heaters, vents, and air conditioning. But few will have any greater impact on the overall physical comfort of captain and crew or the ability of all aboard to enjoy boating throughout the entire season.

REGIONAL CONSIDERATIONS

When considering a new boat which may not have been fully commissioned, the local dealer should be able to make some informed recommendations about the type of heating and/or air conditioning that works well for that particular model in the local climate.

When looking at a used boat, you will ordinarily find systems appropriate for the boat and the local climate, with the important exception of boats which have been relocated from other parts of the country. Boats brought to the Pacific Northwest from Florida or the Gulf Coast may be configured with a special emphasis on cooling the boat rather than warming it up—exactly the opposite of what the Northwest climate calls for (where it isn't unheard of to ward off an early morning chill in July or

August by firing up the heater). Boats headed east from many West Coast ports may have little or no air conditioning aboard, and the heaters may be overspecked for the new climate. In some areas of climatic extremes and subzero winter temperatures, it is customary to haul out and winterize most pleasure boats. Storing a boat ashore between the onset of cold weather and spring eliminates the need for a monster furnace.

BTU'S

Heating and cooling capacities of any system are expressed in BTU's (British thermal units). A rough formula appropriate for all except the most extreme climates states that 15 or 16 BTU's will be needed to control the temperature of each cubic foot of air. A cabin space 8 feet long, 10 feet wide, and 7 feet high would require a capacity of approximately 8,500 BTU's. By determining the BTU capacity of the climate-control equipment on board, a prospective buyer can make an informed guess as to whether the heating and/or air conditioning are up to the task at hand. Some manufacturers or some previous owners may have installed undersized equipment to save money. A unit too small for the job may run so continuously that it becomes worn out prematurely and still fails to provide adequate comfort.

REVERSE-CYCLE AIR CONDITIONING

On medium and larger boats, one of the most popular approaches to comfort control in climates where air conditioning is justified is a reverse-cycle heater and air conditioner. Similar to a household heat pump, the reverse-cycle system uses a condenser, evaporator, and compressor to either extract heat from or transfer heat to seawater. Even cold water contains heat energy. The cooled or heated air is distributed throughout the boat by designated ductwork. Reversible systems often seem to cool a little more effectively than they heat. A reversible system draws as much as 15 amps of 110-volt AC current, so access to a generous amount of shore power or the operation on an on-board AC generation device is essential.

Other Air-Conditioning Options

Air-conditioning systems which are not reversible and are strictly for cooling purposes are also available. Smaller boats on which air conditioning is desired and which lack enough space to contain a built-in system can utilize portable air conditioners which mount in hatchways. A portable system will usually be adequate for cooling about 300 cubic feet below decks.

HEATERS AND FURNACES

Heating a boat can be accomplished by many methods. Dockside, many boaters rely on electric space heaters (either portable or permanently mounted). When a boat is underway or swinging at anchor a number of nonelectrical alternatives are often employed.

Hot-Water Radiators

Hot-water radiators produce free heat underway by circulating hot engine coolant through a heater core and blowing the warmed air around the cabin with a fan. This system is identical in concept to heaters used in automobiles and trucks. There is a practical limitation to the amount of heat which can be extracted from the engine coolant, and a large boat with a single engine might be inadequately heated if relying solely on hot-water radiation based upon the engine's cooling system.

Diesel Furnaces

Diesel fuel is oil-furnace fuel. Diesel-powered boats operating in colder climates frequently are equipped with a diesel furnace. It isn't purely coincidental that some of the more commonly used marine diesel furnaces are marketed by Scandinavian companies. With few moving parts, a diesel furnace can be a low-maintenance and reliable source of fast heat in great abundance. A diesel furnace operates on the vessel's 12-volt system.

Propane Heaters

Propane heaters are not unheard of on boats with other propane appliances such as galley stoves or propane-powered refrigerators. Propane heaters are available in both free-standing or surface-mounted designs.

Free-Standing Fireplaces

Free-standing furnaces and fireplaces can pump out serious amounts of heat and will utilize either solid fuels (wood, coal, wood pellets, etc.) or liquid fuel such as diesel or propane. Free-standing furnaces typically require a generous amount of clearance from combustible material on all sides and a stovepipe-style chimney. Such requirements impose rather unacceptable styling compromises on many designs, and in many boats under 45 feet or so might just use too much space. With a free-standing furnace, sometimes areas nearest the heat source can become uncomfortably warm, while areas farther forward or aft remain inadequately heated. While keeping firewood aboard can present a hassle, on boats of grand enough scale to accommodate a fireplace, there is a certain romantic charm to the notion—although the concept that "fire aboard a boat is usually not a good thing" should not be ignored either.

VENTILATION

Keeping a boat heated or cooled to an agreeable temperature is only part of making a vessel's interior comfortable.
Ventilation is required to remove stale or damp air, galley
steam, bilge and engine-room odors, and to prevent the
accumulation of explosive concentrations of gasoline
vapors or propane. Moisture will build up inside a boat
from human respiration and perspiration and from cooking
and bathing. It will create condensation on cool surfaces
such as windows or the interior of the hull when the air on
board is more humid than the air surrounding a boat. A
complete exchange of air about once an hour is adequate
for normal ventilation and will prevent mold, mildew, and
other general unpleasantness that thrive in damp, inadequately ventilated environments.

If a boat under consideration seems to be inadequately ventilated (a damp mustiness might be the first
clue), additional vents are not too difficult to add. The most
common areas with this need are the galley and the heads.
Increasing a boat's ventilation almost always involves cutting holes in the superstructure or hull of a boat, a task not
wisely undertaken by a new boat owner.

Active and Passive Vents

Vents on a boat are either active (driven by a fan) or passive (such as a clamshell vent positioned to scoop airflow
into the cabin or bilge). Active vents can be driven either
by a boat's 12-volt system or by electricity generated in tiny
solar-electric cells mounted on the external housing of the
vent. Some active vents use both systems, relying on the
sun's energy on brighter days and drawing off the boat's
batteries on cloudy days and after dark. A typical active
vent will circulate between 700 and 1000 cubic feet per
hour when operating at full speed. On gasoline boats,

A possible vent positioned to scoop airflow into the cabin.

engine-room areas will have both passive and active vents. The passive vents insure that no accumulation of explosive vapors occurs when the vessel is underway, and the active vents are used before starting the engine when docked or anchored.

When ventilating a boat it is just as important to consider how to let air out of the boat as it is to bring air aboard. A few passive vents face aft on most boats, with the theory being that as the vessel moves forward a low pressure area is created immediately behind the vent and air from the cabin, engine room, or bilge will flow out of the boat as a result.

Ventilated Lockers

Many boats have doors with integrated louvers on various lockers. These louvers are functional as well as stylish when placed on cabinet doors below sinks in the head and galley, as well as on any locker along the perimeter of the hull. By permitting air flow through these otherwise enclosed spaces, you eliminate the possibility of creating an environment where mold, mildew, odors and rot can breed.

At this point, you've completed an examination of some of the most fundamental systems of a powerboat. If you didn't find a deal-breaking defect that could not be reasonably corrected, it's time to move to other points of interest around the vessel. Should you make an offer on the boat, your surveyor will double- and triple-check everything examined thus far, and as a buyer you will be better prepared to appreciate and interpret any observations the surveyor might make.

It remains important to maintain perspective as the examination of a potential boat continues. Any boat will have compromises in design and execution. So remember, the goal is not to discover a vessel in which no compromise has been made, but rather a boat in which the compromises made are acceptable. For those of us whose personal fortunes inspire us to shop used rather than new, we must also deal with the reality that on the boats we examine most, if not all, of the systems will be partially worn. When considering a used boat it is important to qualify the concept of "partially worn" to differentiate between those things which are in nearly new condition and the things which are nearly (or completely) worn out.

PART THREE

Evaluating the Secondary Systems

THE SECONDARY SYSTEMS are those which are easily changed, replaced, or modified without resorting to a wholesale reconfiguration of the entire boat. Many secondary systems are vitally important to the safe and enjoyable operation of a vessel and deserve the same attention as many of the items considered primary.

20

Anchors and Ground Tackle

THE IMPORTANCE OF THE anchor and anchor line (rode) cannot be overstated. The anchor is called upon to fasten a boat securely to the bottom (often while those aboard are sleeping or have gone ashore in the dinghy) in spite of shifting winds, tides, and currents. If the engine fails, the anchor is often the last line of defense that prevents a boat from washing onto the beach or a rocky reef. The anchor can secure a boat to a fixed, reported position while awaiting help. In hurricane-prone areas, some owners of larger yachts are more comfortable riding out a monster storm at anchor than tied to a fixed dock. With so many vital functions to perform, it is often alarming to observe the large numbers of anchors of dubious suitability mounted on the bow rollers of powerboats.

Almost any anchor will do in calm conditions in a protected harbor. But many boaters discover that their anchor system isn't adequate the first time it faces a stiffer challenge. Unfortunately there is seldom a marine supply store handy in the middle of the night when a 40-knot gale begins to blow. Just because a boat carries an anchor, the first-time powerboat buyer cannot assume that it is of proper design for the intended cruising, or of sufficient size to safely anchor the boat. Cost-cutting manufacturers often supply anchors of minimal capability. And if the previous owner of a boat ever lost an anchor, there's no assurance that it wasn't replaced on the cheap with an insufficiently sized bargain.

PROPER SIZE

Anchors are sized by weight, but it is not weight that holds the boat to the seabed but rather the efficiency with which the anchor digs into the mud, sand, gravel, grass, or catches among rocks on the bottom. Most manufacturers have information regarding the length or tonnage displacement that their various-sized anchors are intended for, and prudent boaters will select one size too large rather than one size too small.

ANCHOR STYLES

Danforth Anchors

Anchor designs today are typically one of three distinct styles: the Danforth, the plow, or the Bruce. Danforth anchors feature two triangular, flat flukes on opposite sides of a central shank. They are very effective in muddy or sandy bottoms where the shovel-like flukes dig in firmly. Danforth anchors are not as reliable on rocky, clay, or grassy bottoms, as the presence of two anchor flukes effectively halves the pressure on each fluke and creates some difficulty in penetrating more resistant surfaces.

Plow Anchors

Plow anchors are typified by a single, pointed fluke similar in shape to an old-fashioned field plow. The shank is often hinged where it connects to the fluke allowing a boat to swing without pulling out of the sea floor. Plow

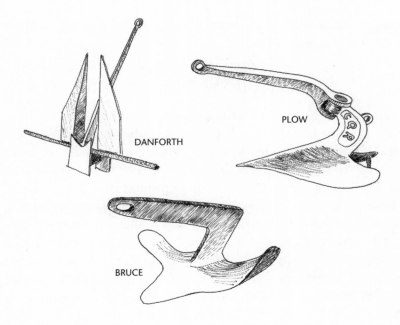

Anchor styles.

anchors are very effective in clay, grass, rocks, and hard-packed mud or sand. Plow anchors are less effective than Danforths in soft mud bottoms since the single fluke takes all of the strain from the anchor rode, and the anchor's greater ability to penetrate a surface can work against its capacity to hold bottom. Perhaps for this reason, most anchor manufacturers specify a plow-style anchor of almost double the weight of a Danforth for the same-sized boat.

Bruce Anchors

Bruce anchors are a one-piece unit with an L-shaped shank and a single, semi-flat, scoop-style fluke of exceptionally abstract geometry. Bruce anchors are very effective on rocky bottoms, as well as clay and hard-packed mud or sand. Bruce anchors are more effective than plow anchors in very soft mud or sand.

NUMBER OF ANCHORS ABOARD

A second anchor is essential to have aboard should the primary anchor become lost or irretrievably stuck on the bottom. Boaters who will be cruising into areas with diverse seabeds are well advised to have two different varieties of anchor. The spare anchor can be deployed from the stern of a boat in crowded harbors to minimize a boat's swinging around the bow anchor and thereby reduce the risk of colliding with nearby boats. When anchoring to ride out a storm, many boaters set two anchors, about 30 degrees to port and starboard of the bow. The load is then evenly divided between the two hooks, and the chances of pulling free are greatly reduced. A boat with a second anchor (particularly if it isn't buried under two hundred pounds of gear in a lazarette) has probably been owned by an experienced sea person.

ANCHOR RODE

The type and length of material used in an anchor rode will determine how easily and securely a vessel can be anchored.

Rode Types by Boat Size

Boats under 25 feet frequently use an all-rope anchor rode. A rode of $3/8"$ diameter is considered adequate for most boats in this size category, but $1/2"$ is better. Medium-sized power boats between 25 and 60 feet often use a combination chain-and-rope rode, with at least one foot of chain per foot of boat length connecting the anchor to the rope. Boats from 25 to 36 feet should use a minimum of $1/2"$ rope (larger is better),

and boats 36 feet and above should use no less than ⅝"
anchor line. Boats over 60 feet almost always use an all-
chain rode. As anchor chain will often weigh a pound or
more per foot, a few hundred feet of all chain rode stowed
in the bow has a significant effect on the sea-keeping abilities of a small- to medium-sized powerboat.

Rode Length and Available Scope

Length of anchor rode becomes important when considering the concept of scope, the relationship between the
amount of anchor rode deployed and the depth of the
water. Anchors are most secure when the pull of the boat
against the anchor is as close to horizontal as possible.
Under ideal conditions, it is wise to use five to seven times
as much anchor rode as the depth of an anchorage at high
tide. Seasoned boaters remember to include the height of
the anchor roller above the waterline when calculating
depth. Anchoring in a crowded harbor on a holiday weekend may require a boater to compromise between enough

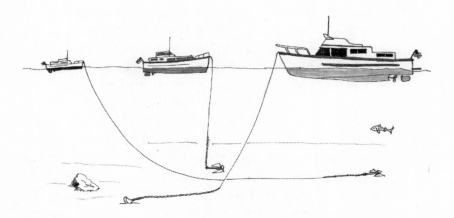

*Length of anchor rode becomes important when considering the
concept of scope.*

scope to hold bottom in practically any condition and reduced scope to minimize the swinging arc as wind and/or tide changes. An all-chain rode can often hold effectively at a 3:1 or 4:1 scope, great for crowded conditions or for anchoring in a fjord-style inlet with deep water right up to the shoreline. While most boaters won't find themselves in situations where 300 feet or more of anchor rode is required, it is better to have it and not need it than to ever need it and not have it. When examining an anchor locker, it is common to see brightly colored plastic strips attached to an anchor rode in various places. The previous owner has marked the rode at regular intervals to indicate the amount of rode payed out in anchoring, a worthwhile effort indeed. By consulting a chart or asking experienced boaters, the first-time boat buyer can find out the range of depths at typical local anchorages (as well as the daily tidal ranges) to determine whether the vessel contains enough rode.

ANCHOR LOCKERS

While the anchor is typically stowed on deck, the rope and/or chain will stow below deck in the anchor locker. Some anchor lockers are only accessible from the deck, while others may be opened below decks and accessed horizontally. Below-deck access allows a spare hand to stack or coil the rode as the anchor is retrieved and minimize the chance of any tangles during the next anchor setting. Anchor lockers are easier to maintain if there is a drain incorporated into the design. Mud, sand, and bits of seaweed and shell brought aboard by the chain portion of the rode in particular tend to dry up and fall into the bottom of the locker, and there will be some water brought into the locker by a wet rode as well. A drain connecting the anchor locker to the bilge or routing the drainage overboard near the waterline at the bow has obvious utility.

ANCHOR ROLLERS AND WINDLASSES

For deploying and recovering, anchor rollers and wind-lasses are both important items. Anchor rollers, mounted on bow pulpits, allow an anchor to be raised or lowered with reduced risk of banging into the hull. The rollers also provide a smooth surface for the anchor rode to rest against when the anchor is deployed, reducing chafing which weakens the rode. If forced to retrieve an anchor by hand, anchor rollers allow a horizontal pull of the rode across the deck to be converted to a vertical lifting of the anchor so that boaters can pull with their legs rather than with their backs!

No boater who anchors a boat of any appreciable size would want to be without a windlass, either manual or electric. Windlasses are literally winding tools that allow a boater to use the laws of physics rather than brute strength to haul an anchor. The manual variety are oper-ated with either a crank or a lever with the anchor rode wrapped around a drum, while the electric type use a motor similar to an automotive starting motor to turn the drum and recover the anchor. The most versatile wind-lasses incorporate both a drum (capstan) for hauling rope and a gypsy (a set of cogged teeth on a wheel) to haul chain. Smaller boats often have no room for a windlass, but with shallower drafts allowing anchoring in shallower depths and lighter-weight anchors being sufficient to hold lighter craft, most adults can haul the anchors involved unassisted.

OTHER ANCHOR CONSIDERATIONS

Rarely found on boats is a wash-down system with which a boater, using a short length of hose connected to a fitting near the windlass, can blast mud from an anchor chain before it comes across the bow roller (thereby eliminating most of the muddy buildup in the anchor locker and on the foredeck). Adequate deck space in the anchor area and a decent safety rail will be appreciated by a boater attempting to deploy or retrieve an anchor in rough seas or on a rain-slickened deck. Some boats feature a samson post at the bow to tie off the anchor rode, but a minimum of one heavy-duty cleat will also suffice.

21

Food Storage and Refrigeration

NEEDS VARY WIDELY with regard to food storage and refrigeration. Whether the goal is to keep a six-pack and a picnic lunch cold for a half-day fishing trip or to adequately provision for a crew of 8 to 10 on a two-week offshore cruise, some prepurchase evaluation of the boat's systems and capacities for storing fresh, frozen, or packaged food will yield genuine benefits.

ICE CHESTS

For small day cruisers, a portable ice chest might be all of the food storage required. An ice chest is inexpensive to acquire, will demand very little maintenance, and uses no electricity. When secured by deck braces, a stoutly built ice chest can additionally justify its space on a small boat by doubling as another seat. Some enterprising manufacturers sell seat cushions designed to be used atop an ice chest. An ice chest is also useful aboard a boat with a small built-in refrigerator, when temporary demands (such as entertaining a larger-than-normal crowd) exceed the regular capacity for cold storage.

TWELVE-VOLT REFRIGERATOR/FREEZER COMBOS

Boaters who spend quite a bit of time at various city marinas, or whose cruising habits involve being anchored out for no more than a few days, will be sufficiently served by a 12-volt/110-volt refrigerator/freezer unit. These popular coolers operate either from the 12-volt DC power of the onboard batteries, or by converting available 110-volt AC shore power to 12-volt DC and not taxing the house batteries. The most popular sizes of these built-in units are approximately three cubic feet and six cubic feet. When operating from the house batteries, these refrigeration units draw about one amp per cubic foot per hour (and will actively run about 30 minutes per hour). So the operation of a six-cubic-foot refrigerator/freezer for 48 hours can consume the entire 150-amp recommended maximum discharge of a 300-amp battery. If nothing but the refrigerator were drawing down the house battery, it would be smart to start a generator or run the main engine for a period of time sufficient to recharge the battery every couple of days. Cabin lights, water pumps, radios, heater and vent fans, anchor lights, and so forth usually share the power of the same battery running the refrigerator. In most cases when anchored out with 300 amps or less of house-battery capacity and a six-cubic-foot refrigerator/freezer combo, it is advisable to run a generator or main engine for a brief period everyday to replenish the house-battery bank. On a used boat with this type of refrigerator, make sure that the original unit has not been replaced on the cheap with something from an RV supply store. Appliances sold for use in motor homes are not suitable for a boat as they usually are not constructed from material with adequate corrosion resistance.

Ice Is Nice

Refrigerator/freezer combinations are very popular because they are similar in concept and appearance to home refrigerators. Other than their fairly inefficient use of power, the only serious compromise with these appliances is the paltry freezer capacity, particularly on the smaller sizes. Boaters who entertain a lot and operate an active bar would have a difficult time counting on the combo refrigerator/freezer to provide a reliable quantity of ice. A number of manufacturers build 110-volt AC icemakers which are handy when dockside (or when the generator is running) for keeping the drinks cool or creating a chestful of ice to store the catch of the day until dinner time.

ICEBOXES AND HOLDING PLATES

Built-in iceboxes are found on some older boats and on boats where the accommodations for passengers and crew are extensive enough that a typical refrigerator would not be sufficient to keep a logical amount of food cold. Iceboxes are seldom cooled with ice. Very high efficiency cooling systems known as holding plates can, in a well-insulated ice box, create temperatures as low as -20 degrees Fahrenheit.

A holding plate's compressor may be powered electrically and/or driven hydraulically by the boat's engine. Seawater can be pumped through the cooling machinery to more effectively transfer the heat, but many simply transfer the heat removed from the icebox into the bilge, cabin, or outside air. Engine-driven systems may need to be operated for only an hour or two per day to maintain adequate refrigeration.

OTHER REFRIGERATION OPTIONS

Larger boats with all-electric galleys and onboard generators often have a standard household-sized refrigerator that operates on AC only. On boats with propane, there are some thermoelectric refrigeration systems which are propane driven. Many of these systems are a three-way affair, combining the possibility of propane-generated power with the options of 12-volt battery or 110-volt AC operation.

THE FREON QUESTION

To prepare yourself for an eventual expense or to discover that there is one less thing to be concerned about, determine if possible what type of refrigerant gas is used aboard. For decades the standard refrigerant gas was R-12, but due to concerns that R-12 (freon) is a major contributor to the reduction of ozone in the earth's upper atmosphere, the manufacture of R-12 has been, by law, discontinued in most countries in the 1990s. Refrigerators using R-12 are still legal to own and operate, but when being serviced a technician must take special precautions to capture any freon which might need to be vented from the system. The captured refrigerant is then processed, filtered, and recycled into other refrigerators which need a recharge of coolant. Since freon is no longer manufactured and some R-12 will inevitably escape into the atmosphere through leaky fittings and so forth, the supply of R-12 is disappearing faster than the refrigerators which require it are wearing out. So, freon is scarce and expensive. Many systems originally designed for R-12 can be fairly inexpensively converted to utilize one of the more modern, alternative gases available. New boats, or boats where the refrigeration has been upgraded since 1996, ordinarily use a refrigerant such as HFC-134A which does an excellent job of absorbing heat and at least so far has not been found to have any damaging effects on the atmosphere.

CANNED, PACKAGED, AND FREEZE-DRIED STORAGE

The galley lockers on most boats require the cruising chef to rely on a basic selection of cooking utensils. To accommodate sufficient storage for canned and packaged foods in a fairly compact area, many of the specialized pans and appliances taken for granted in the kitchen ashore need to be replaced by a few highly versatile items. If there just doesn't seem to be enough storage space in the galley, there are probably a number of places aboard where canned, packaged or freeze-dried foods can be stored for extended periods, to be brought to the galley every few days.

22

Galley Stoves
and Fuel Systems

COOKING APPLIANCES ON BOATS are most commonly
fueled by alcohol or propane, or use electricity.
Cooking units in the marine environment will quite
often feature stainless rails around the perimeter of the
cook top or some other system to keep pots of boiling
water from sliding off in a beam sea or when the boat
encounters a large wake.

ALCOHOL STOVES

Small boats commonly use a two- or three-burner alcohol stove, with liquid alcohol being stored in a reser-
voir and used to create controlled flames for heat. With
any type of open-flame system, owners of gasoline-
powered boats must be especially cautious that there is
no buildup of gasoline vapors in the bilge while the
stove is in operation. Most boats with alcohol stoves
are under 28 feet and properly designed to provide an
adequate ventilation for safe operation of an alcohol
stove.

ELECTRIC GALLEY RANGES

Larger boats with onboard generators often use a three- or four-burner electric cook top and oven combination. These marine versions of an electric range operate on 110-volt AC power at sea, and some may also adapt to 220-volt AC when connected to an ample supply of dockside power. A generator producing ample AC current is required to operate an electric galley range when anchored or underway.

DIESEL COOKSTOVES

Diesel cookstoves are not unknown, but while somewhat commonplace on tugs or commercial fishing boats, their use is pretty unusual on pleasure boats. A diesel stove uses a flame to heat an iron stove-plate and the exhaust is piped directly out of the boat.

PROPANE STOVES AND SYSTEMS

On many boats, galley stoves are fueled by propane (Liquefied Petroleum Gas). Space heaters, deck-rail barbecues, and thermoelectric refrigerators may be powered by propane as well.

Safety Concerns

Propane is a flammable gas which is heavier than air. Any propane which enters a boat (and is not burned) gravitates into the bilge. When properly installed, maintained, and operated, propane systems are of no particular safety concern on most boats, but some prudent mariners resist the use of propane stoves on gasoline-powered boats. Gasoline vapors can conceivably be ignited by the open flame of a propane burner or oven unit, and propane vapors collecting in the bilge can create an explosive condition if ignited by stray current from an engine's electrical ignition system.

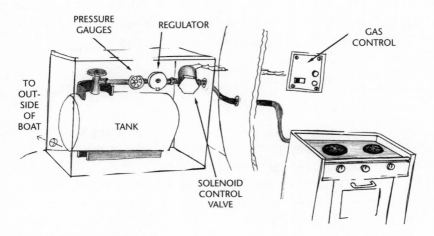

A propane system.

Propane Lockers

Propane tanks should be mounted in a dedicated locker on the exterior of the boat. Some boats have propane tanks secured directly to the deck or superstructure without benefit of a container to protect the tanks and valve assemblies from the elements or the possibility of damage from accidental impact. Propane lockers should open directly to open air, and not be located below decks, in a lazarette, or other enclosed area. Propane lockers should be vented from the bottom (remember *heavier* than air), with the vent line running overboard to a point above the waterline but no closer than a couple of feet from any engine, stove, or furnace exhaust ports.

Valves and Solenoids

All propane systems need a shut-off solenoid in the locker to allow the flow of gas to be stopped remotely from the galley by means of an electric switch. It isn't always practical to close or open the main propane tank valves each time an appliance is turned off or on, but most boaters will shut off the manual tank valves when securing the vessel for the night.

Propane Lines

On a used boat, it can be important to be sure that there have not been any post-manufacture splices made in the propane fuel lines. Each propane appliance should have an individual, unbroken fuel line running directly to it from the propane locker. T-fittings are acceptable as part of the plumbing assembly exiting the propane tanks, but no other joints should be made "downstream" from this point. Most manufacturers would never consider running a propane line through the bilge or engine room, and it might be wise to determine that a former owner hasn't routed a line through these areas during a previous renovation.

Sniffers

Every boat with propane aboard should have a gas-detecting sniffer installed in the bilge. The sniffer should be connected to a loud audio alarm and may also connect to the electric solenoid control in the propane locker. Most sniffers will have a test position so that a boater can determine that the sniffer is operational and be familiar with the sound of the sniffer's alarm.

23

Engine Instrumentation

ENGINE INSTRUMENTATION ALLOWS the boater to monitor the vital signs of a vessel's power plant and thereby helps assure reliable operation.

ANALOG VS. DIGITAL

Each helm station should have a number of important instruments in working condition. Instrumentation on modern powerboats may be either analog type with needle-and-dial readouts or the digital style with lighted numeric displays. Analog instruments in particular should be backlit for visibility at night, and digital instruments should have a brightness control for the same purpose. Many experienced boaters prefer analog instruments since there is a lower chance of a false reading due to electronic malfunction. Automotive-type idiot lights—as in "you just fried the engine, idiot"—have no place aboard a boat, unless they are redundant to a standard digital or analog gauge.

ENGINE ALARMS

On multiple-engine boats, each engine must have a complete set of gauges and instruments. As a backup system to the engine instrumentation, a boat should have an engine alarm for each engine (with an alarm indicator at each helm) to alert an otherwise distracted boater that the engine oil pressure has dropped to a dangerous level or that the coolant is becoming overheated. Some boats incorporate other warnings such as "bilge flooding" into the alarm system.

THREE ESSENTIAL GAUGES

The most important trio of instruments on a powerboat are the temperature gauge, the oil-pressure gauge, and the tachometer. As you become familiar with your vessel, you'll begin to recognize the normal temperature and oil-pressure readings associated with various engine speeds. If the temperature or oil-pressure readings begin to vary the wise mariner will waste little time before determining why. A clogged raw-water intake can cause radical overheating of a marine engine in a matter of minutes. Noticing a climbing temperature before the engine alarm sounds may well make the difference between shutting down long enough to clear the water intake or shutting down long enough to rebuild an engine! A severed oil-return line from the turbo to the crankcase (or similar condition) will show up as a steadily decreasing oil-pressure reading long before the pressure gets low enough to seriously damage the engine. On twin-engine vessels, the readings between both engines should be very close to identical for temperature and oil pressure at any given rpm. Any abnormal indicators can be the earliest warning of impending problems.

When underway, experienced boaters avoid letting more than a minute or so elapse between glances at the engine instrumentation.

FUEL GAUGES

Fuel gauges are also important, but a large percentage of boaters place very little trust in them. They prefer to calculate remaining fuel by subtracting the amount of fuel used since the last fill-up (engine hours x average gallons/hour fuel consumption) from the tankage available. Seasoned boaters know how many engine hours have been accumulated at the last refueling and have a predetermined hour reading by which time they plan to refuel. Fuel-gauge indicators may bounce through a wide range when a planing hull is pounding through whitecaps, and there is always the possibility that the sending unit could become stuck in any fuel tank. A fuel gauge is an excellent backup to a disciplined awareness of the amount of fuel aboard.

VOLTMETERS

Voltmeters monitor the effectiveness of a boat's charging system when the engine is running, as well as the level to which a battery bank has been charged or discharged when the engine is not running. A properly functioning alternator will create readings of 14-15 volts when cruising. Readings consistently under 12 volts are the first indication of a failed alternator, a broken drive belt, or something amiss with the wiring or the batteries.

SPEEDOMETERS

Many boats have been built without speedometers aboard. The typical marine speedometer (speed log) uses a paddlewheel device which protrudes through the hull and turns at a rate which changes with the speed of the vessel through water. The inaccuracies occur because the water itself beneath the boat is commonly moving as well due to tidal or river currents. A boat achieving 12 knots through the water with a 4-knot current will actually be making 16 knots for navigational purposes. An oncoming boat in the same current with an identical 12-knot speedometer reading will in reality be achieving a speed over the bottom of only 8 knots. Boaters tend to rely more on the knowledge that "at 1800 rpm this boat makes 10 knots before wind or current considerations" than on speedometer readings, and will be aware of the speed and direction of prevailing currents where they are cruising. On boats with GPS or Loran systems (see "Electronics and Navigation Aids," next chapter) the SOG (speed-over-ground) readings are far more useful and accurate than a marine speedometer.

ENGINE-HOUR METERS

An engine-hour meter on a boat performs many of the same functions as an odometer does in a car. Hour meters report the number of hours on an engine and are useful in scheduling service intervals and refueling stops. Unlike an automotive odometer, there aren't strict federal sanctions regarding changing hour meter readings. By the same token, there are ordinarily not a lot of boats around where any engine-hour fraud has taken place. When an engine is replaced with a *new, never previously* run engine, an argument with some merit can be made for replacing the hour meter with a fresh unit that reads zero. But many boaters prefer to simply make a note in the maintenance log, recording the date and hour reading when an engine is changed. Maintaining the original hour meter will help track the hours on related equipment such as transmissions, pumps, or alternators which may have been transferred from an old engine to the new.

Some boats have had the hour meters replaced when an engine has been subjected to a major overhaul. If considering a used boat with a replaced hour meter following an overhaul, press for a complete documentation of the work done, and consult a marine engine mechanic for a second opinion as to the actual extent of the work. A note in the maintenance log that reads "3655 hours...rebuilt injector pump, injectors, ground the valves, replaced the head gasket, replaced the oil and fuel pumps and the raw-water pump" is a more ethical and accurate method of recording the periodic rejuvenation of an engine than installing a zero-reading hour meter and claiming a major overhaul.

Mismatched Hour Meters

When considering a twin-engine boat, it can be important to note any differences between the readings on the hour meters. A difference of under a hundred hours on a used boat with a thousand or more engine hours is probably not significant and may represent nothing more serious than time spent trolling for fish or an incident where a prop was lost halfway between two remote ports and the engine shut down until a replacement was obtained. For example, if two engines have readings of "2400 hours" and "50 hours" (and the 50-hour reading is explained because the starboard engine has been recently replaced), it is not ridiculous to question whether the port engine might be approaching the end of its career as well. The new engine may have been required due to some incident which wouldn't necessarily affect the other engine, such as the sudden loss of coolant or lubrication. The new engine may have been installed due to a condition such as insufficient maintenance or accumulated general wear, and either is likely to have affected the remaining engine as well. What's causing the current owner to place the boat on the market so soon after replacing one engine? It could be purely coincidental, but you should proceed with eyes wide open and a thorough mechanical survey.

OIL-TEMPERATURE GAUGES

A useful gauge not always found on powerboats is an oil-temperature gauge. Being aware of oil temperature is particularly helpful when operating a turbo-charged diesel engine. The turbo will benefit from the oil being slightly warmed before the engine reaches a speed where the turbo becomes active, and it is good practice to allow the engine oil to cool a little below its normal operating temperature before shutting a turbo-diesel engine down. Boaters with turbo-diesel powerplants needn't rely strictly on an oil-temperature gauge. Operational practices like allowing the engine to warm up before taking off and to cool down a few minutes before hitting the stop switch accomplish the goal without a gauge. Oil coolers are an important item on many marine engines, turbo charged or not, and an oil-temperature gauge can be an early indicator of a malfunctioning oil-cooling system.

On a boat equipped with an AC generator, it is important to have, at the helm, at least an oil-pressure and temperature gauge for the gen-set motor as well.

24

Electronics and Navigation Aids

B OATING HAS BECOME COMPUTERIZED. The array of electronics available to the pleasure boater today for satellite navigation and charting purposes is more informative than anything aboard a billion-dollar ocean liner a couple of decades ago. The downside of all of the electronic flash and dazzle is that one does not simply "reboot" after hitting a rock ("reboat" might be a more accurate term).

CHARTS AND COMPASS ARE STILL ESSENTIAL

Boaters should regard the electronic conveniences as accessories to, rather than substitutes for, traditional chart and compass navigation. The regulations requiring boaters to have adequate charts for their cruising area and to refer to those charts during navigation have not been suspended or modified in response to the numerous computerized charting systems now available. In the event of an accident, failure to use official charts could conceivably create a situation in which insurance coverage is denied. Look for adequate space at the helm station to lay out a chart and some provision to keep it flat, dry, and secure from wind. A well-calibrated compass at the wheel is essential as well. Many boats are now equipped with electronic compasses, but at least one compass aboard should be a traditional, liquid-filled, card-style compass. The earth's magnetic field is infinitely more reliable than any solid-state circuitry ever invented.

VHF RADIO

An electronic item which must be considered an absolute essential on any powerboat is a VHF (Very High Frequency) radio. The VHF is a boater's tool for contacting other boats in the area, listening to NOAA weather forecasts, and communicating with the Coast Guard or a private tow service in case of emergency. Boats operated solely in U.S. waters no longer need to obtain an FCC license for VHF radios (a license is required for U.S. boaters broadcasting in many foreign countries, including Canada), but strict regulations as well as customary courtesies must be observed when operating a VHF. One VHF at each helm should provide adequate redundancy, and boaters with only one helm should consider carrying a second, hand-held VHF as an emergency backup. Boats operating in offshore conditions where a liferaft is advisable often keep a VHF in the raft's survival equipment as well.

Many VHF radios incorporate a hailing feature which allows the operator to broadcast through an externally mounted speaker and communicate directly with fuel-dock attendants, line handlers, or nearby boaters without a VHF radio. On some of the upper-end VHF units, a provision for generating fog horn signals through the hailing speaker at regular intervals can make safe operation slightly easier in restricted visibility. Boaters who operate more than 10 or 15 miles from shore will require a longer antenna so that the boat can pick up signals originating on land despite the curvature of the earth.

FATHOMETERS

In addition to a VHF radio, another must for safe operation of a powerboat is a fathometer or depth sounder. A depth sounder is not a substitute for knowing one's position on a chart and the indicated depth in that location, but it is an indispensable supplement. A depth sounder can also help establish a boat's position when operating in dense fog or darkness by comparing depth changes in the water below the keel to recorded depth changes on a chart. Virtually all depth sounders manufactured in the last several years are digital units which display a number representing feet, meters, or fathoms between the depth-sounding transducer's (the sensor's) position on the hull and the sea floor. When navigating through shallow waters it is important to remember that the displayed number represents less than the actual clearance between the hull and the bottom when a hull component, such as a keel, extends below the point where the transducer is mounted. Many fathometers incorporate a video display which informs a boater about the shape of the bottom contour, the temperature of the water at the transducer, and the presence or absence of fish in the area. An alarm feature on most depth sounders will alert a skipper when the depth drops below a predetermined minimum or exceeds a predetermined maximum. Such an alarm may call attention to an error in navigation or to a dragging anchor in time to take corrective action and avoid serious consequences. Boats with more than one helm station should have a fathometer at each.

GPS

GPS (Global Positioning System) receivers have become commonplace on boats. By receiving signals from a group of satellites orbiting the earth and comparing the strength of their signals, a GPS receiver calculates with astonishing accuracy the speed, course, and precise longitude and latitude of a vessel. In the interest of national security, the U.S. government tweaks the GPS signals so that recreational boaters or terrorist missile launchers can only receive signals accurate to within about 100 yards or so. GPS should never be relied upon for charting a course very near shore or through a restricted channel. GPS accuracy can be improved by purchasing a differential GPS that supposedly gives a more accurate reading by receiving an additional signal from a land-based transmitter which corrects the signal from the federal detuning. Apparently we must only hope that missile-launching terrorists don't invest the extra dollars in the differential system.

GPS Plotters

GPS signals are used by electronic charting devices which can produce a video screen facsimile of a nautical chart and indicate a vessel's position thereon. These plotters are becoming increasingly popular and more affordable, and provide an excellent tool for confirming your navigational accuracy when using official government charts.

AUTOPILOTS

Autopilots should never be used as a substitute for maintaining a constant lookout.

Autopilots are a popular feature for boaters who make long runs in open water. When a course has been set and the autopilot adjusted and activated, a skipper need not keep a hand on the wheel at all times. Autopilots should never substitute for maintaining a constant lookout when underway, since the autopilot is unable to detect and avoid other boats, fish nets, or floating debris. Even the most veteran boaters have an occasional incident of miscalculated position, and the first indication that the boat isn't where it was thought to be is usually that landmarks and buoys do not somehow look right. A boat steaming along with all aboard eating dinner in the saloon is an impending disaster. Autopilots perform a valuable task by often allowing a boat to steer a straighter course than most helmsmen could accomplish unassisted. Many of the newer autopilots will interface with a plotter to allow a boater to program course changes for the autopilot at predetermined positions.

LORAN

Some used boats will be equipped with Loran-C. Loran is a navigational system similar to GPS but uses dedicated radio signals broadcast from land instead of orbiting satellites. Loran units have not been in general manufacture since the mid-1990s, when the U.S. government concluded that the GPS system was reliable enough to replace it. Sometime early in the 21st century the Loran-C plug will be pulled, and Loran-C receivers will become obsolete.

RADAR

Radar is very useful for navigation after dark or in foggy conditions. In coastal and inland areas, the image of the shoreline will appear on the radar screen and assist a mariner in getting his bearings and determining position on the appropriate chart. Most radar displays have a range feature showing approximate distance from any radar target displayed, and this is also extremely helpful in charting a vessel's position and course. While GPS will produce a sufficiently accurate position for charting purposes, radar allows a boater to visually detect nearby boats, buoys, etc. and avoid a possible collision. Radar is more costly than a standard GPS receiver, but if a boater can afford only one system, radar takes priority in most situations. When considering a boat with radar, note whether the radar antenna is mounted in such a manner that people on deck or on the fly bridge will not be exposed to potentially harmful radiation while the radar is in use. Radar should never be operated in crowded areas like marinas, fuel docks, or locks to avoid exposing anybody to the radiation emitted.

RECREATIONAL ELECTRONICS

Recreational electronics aboard most vessels include a stereo system, with the stereo components being largely a matter of personal preference. Buyers should note whether a marine stereo system has been installed. Most typical automobile stereo systems don't hold up well in the marine environment.

Many CD players tend to skip in moderate or heavier seas, so cassette tapes remain very popular among music-loving boaters. As the size of the required receivers has been reduced to a workable level, more boaters are installing satellite TV receivers.

CB Radios, Phones, and Computers

Additional electronics often found on boats include CB radios and cellular phones, neither of which is an adequate substitute for a VHF radio. Small portable computers are finding their way aboard in increasing frequency to handle such chores as vessel record keeping and assisting in navigation. Very *deluxe* boats often incorporate direct satellite-link telephone systems, allowing a boater to place a phone call to virtually any telephone on the planet from any place the vessel happens to be.

Intercoms

On boats with a fly bridge, an intercom to communicate between the bridge and the main saloon can eliminate a lot of the yelling, thumping on the cabintop, or scrambling up and down from the bridge. Another handy onboard communication system which a boater might want to acquire soon after purchasing a boat is a set of two or more hands-free, headband-style walkie-talkies. For the first several dozen dockings with a newly acquired boat, the helmsman and the deck crew will be developing an understanding of how the boat behaves in different types of close quarters and learning to work together to dock safely and gracefully. The docking process can be stressful enough without having to shout at one another in order to be heard above the engines. A few important comments such as "you're coming in way too fast, reverse!" successfully communicated by the walkie-talkies will quickly justify the modest investment in the devices.

25

Dinghies and Davits

FOR MOST BOATS LARGER Than 24 feet or so, the prospective boat buyer has two boats to consider: the primary vessel and the dinghy. When considering a used boat, it is important to clarify with the listing broker or the owner whether or not any dinghy on board at the time of inspection is included in the sale. Ditto for any outboard motors which may be attached to a dinghy or stowed elsewhere. If not specifically included in the vessel's listing manifest, it may not be the seller's intention to include them.

RIGID-HULL DINGHIES

Experienced boaters have preferences for various types of dinghies, with the two general categories consisting of rigid and inflatable hulls. Rigid-hull dinghies are usually built of fiberglass or aluminum rather than wood, and some are even constructed by molding thick plastic. Rigid-hull dinghies are easier to row than most inflatables, and can have higher freeboard to help keep the dinghy and its occupants dry if the water gets choppy. The higher freeboard also makes a rigid dinghy better for towing on a line between anchorages, since it is less likely to be swamped by a large wave or wake. If a dinghy must be dragged across a gravelly beach, a rigid hull will withstand such treatment far better than an inflatable (although the inflatable may be light enough to carry, anyway). Rigid-hull dinghies can handle a higher horsepower outboard than similar-sized inflatables. Disadvantages to rigid-hull dinghies include heavier weight, the reduced number of options for stowing aboard the boat, and the potential to damage the mother ship's hull as the dinghy knocks against it while loading or unloading passengers and supplies.

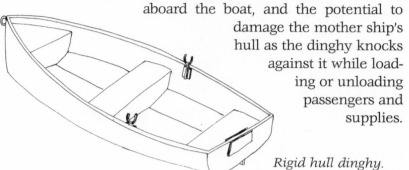

Rigid hull dinghy.

INFLATABLE DINGHIES

Inflatable dinghies are usually lighter in weight than a well-constructed rigid hull of similar size. Inflatables are virtually unsinkable so long as the integrity of the air chambers is intact. An inflatable boat filled completely with water is still buoyant and can be bailed out, although flotation of an inflatable or any boat when swamped is affected by the weight of any nonbuoyant items aboard (such as an outboard). Some inflatables have no detectable keel and can be difficult to row or to maintain course with an outboard (some models attempt to resolve this problem with an inflatable keel). Hybrid inflatables combine an inflatable boat and a rigid fiberglass hull. Modern inflatable boats are built of extremely tough materials and durable construction techniques, but the possibility of a disastrous puncture can never be eliminated. Inflatables dinghies can be deflated and rolled up to a fairly compact size, creating some alternatives for stowing that would not be possible with a rigid hull. Inflatable dinghies should not be operated

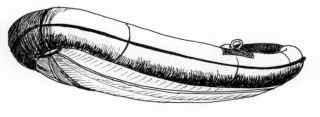

Hybrid inflatables combine an inflatable boat and a rigid fiberglass hull.

at the highest speeds obtainable with a rigid hull. Due to light-weight design and because it rides high in the water, an inflatable with only one person aboard operating an outboard in the stern can be susceptible to flipping backwards when a stout wind gets under the bow.

LAUNCHING, RECOVERING, AND STOWING DINGHIES

Most boats have systems for launching and recovering a dinghy and for stowing it. Some trawler-style yachts incorporate mast-and-boom systems with compound blocks (pulleys). Some larger boats use an electric crane with a swiveling arm to pick the dinghy up from the water and swing it aboard onto chocks on the boat deck. Many boaters mount a dinghy vertically on the swim step and use a line from the transom to control raising or lowering from the fulcrum point created by the swim step attachments. (On many boats the white stern running light is obscured when the dinghy is up on the swim step davits and should be relocated to make the boat safe and legal.) Another system on many boats relies on manual or electric winching to hoist the dinghy, on a bridle, up the transom of the boat to be left suspended there during transit.

PART FOUR

Let's Make a Deal

AFTER EVALUATING YOUR PLANS for the boat's usage, prioritizing your wants and wishes, taking the budget into consideration, and examining a boat thoroughly to appreciate the strengths and weaknesses of its design as well as the type and condition of its equipment...*have you found the perfect boat?* Most likely not, but you may have found the "right" boat, all the same.

26

Drawing Conclusions

UNLESS A BOAT IS BRAND NEW, it is realistic to expect that some of the systems aboard will be suffering from wear and tear. Most boats are cosmetically perfect for about the first ten minutes of the first cruise. Any problems turned up through preliminary inspection should be evaluated as to the potential cost to remedy or replace. Obviously there's a great degree of difference between "the curtains in the galley are stained" and "the starboard fuel tank is leaking." Even a boat with a serious problem might be a good candidate, if the problem is an isolated situation on an otherwise decent boat, and the seller will agree to have it professionally repaired as a condition of sale (or allow an adequate price adjustment to enable the buyer to have it repaired). Frequently buyers use most of their cash for the down payment on a financed boat. So it is more practical to have the seller make the repair than reduce the price, since the buyer may be financially inconvenienced to have to pay for a repair immediately upon closing the deal.

FEELINGS ARE IMPORTANT, TOO

Buying a boat is a bit like getting married: it can be a long-term commitment and an expensive situation to undo!

Make certain to listen to your heart as well as to your head when deciding whether or not to make an offer on a specific boat. Even if a boat passes muster on all of the major points on a checklist, it's important to consider how well you simply like the boat. A common folktale describes a landlubber asking an old seafarer, "How do you know if you've bought the right boat?" The old seafarer replies, "When I get in my dinghy and pull for shore and look back at her...if she calls out to me and I feel like my heart is anchored right out there with her, then that's the right boat."

Spouses and partners who will be part of the boat-buying process and boat-owning experience must be encouraged to express themselves without reservation during the selection phase. Nothing can ruin the boating experience more than a spouse or partner announcing on the second or third cruise "I hate the boat, can't understand how it was ever purchased in the first place, and never plan to go out on it again."

27

Making an Offer

IF DESIGN AND CONCEPT ARE RIGHT, the subject-to-survey condition seems okay, and your significant other likes the boat, the time may have arrived to make an offer.

ELEMENTS OF AN OFFER

An offer to purchase a boat can be structured a number of different ways. The more elaborate and costly the vessel, the more complex the offer is likely to be. "I'll give you six hundred dollars for your dinghy" is technically an offer to purchase a boat and is probably completely appropriate for a transaction of that magnitude. An offer to purchase a megamillion-dollar commercial passenger vessel may be half an inch of paper thick and require a couple of attorneys.

For most recreational boats the offer will have the following characteristics: be in writing; indicate a price the purchaser is willing to pay; and state that the offer is subject to sea trial, survey, and acceptable financing. An offer will usually be accompanied by a cash deposit, and this "earnest money" will revert to the seller and/or broker should the buyer refuse, without good cause, to complete the sale.

ABOUT PRICE

There is seldom a reason to agree to pay the full asking price of a new or used boat. Exceptions do occur, of course. If you've done enough shopping to discover that a used boat which has just entered the market is seriously underpriced, with a number of interested buyers sniffing around, it can be better to settle for an excellent deal on the right boat than to lose out by pressing for a miracle deal instead.

New Boat Prices

Determining the price to offer can be approached from at least a semi-informed standpoint. New boats from production manufacturers will often have 20-30 percent or more markup incorporated into the list price. When buying a boat, it's seldom appropriate to adopt the "show me your invoice and I'll give you another hundred dollars" approach that seems so prevalent in the new-car market. Some larger-volume new-car dealers might sell 30-50 new cars in a weekend, while many boat dealers would be ecstatic to sell eight new boats in a month. Profit isn't a dirty word, but rather the ingredient in the economic mix which allows a dealer to provide outstanding customer service. Some buyers of large-ticket items get too distracted by trying to determine how much profit the dealer is making (vs. how much profit they believe the dealer's entitled to). They should be more interested in paying a fair price and receiving competent, professional service.

Many new boats are priced with enough of a fudge factor to allow the broker to flatter, with an inflated trade-in value, the ego of a buyer who owns an older boat. A first-time buyer doesn't have a trade-in and shouldn't be expected to foot the bill for those who do.

Out-of-Town Dealers

There are a number of excellent ways to obtain a general feel for a fair price on a new boat. A phone call to an out-of-town broker may give you additional insight on prices at which a boat might be available. Some out-of-town brokers may roll out the old "sorry, we don't price over the phone" routine, but many will be willing to discuss a serious discount on a particular make and model to give a prospective buyer an incentive to make the trip to their location. There's a good chance that a boat buyer who lives in Whoville and calls a broker in Slipknot may be given a very good price. (Maybe even the same price that a buyer from Slipknot might have been quoted by the Whoville brokerage with the situation reversed!) It is almost always preferable to buy from, and establish rapport with, the local broker.

Boat Show Specials

Boat Show Specials can offer fairly decent values, but it would be a mistake to assume that the boat show price is always the absolutely best available deal. A yacht broker displaying and selling boats in a boat show is aware that all competitors will be at the same show and marketing to the same bargain-hunting customers. Many of the sale prices at boat shows are about as low as the yacht broker is willing to go without a little more incentive (such as a ready and willing buyer seriously offering something even slightly less).

Asking the Bank

Price research may be effectively conducted at the local bank. The bank may very well provide inventory financing for a boat dealer and know exactly what the wholesale cost of various boats are, but don't expect the bank to share this confidential information with you. Helping you make an informed buy on a boat wouldn't be worth alienating the yacht broker and his multimillion-dollar inventory loan. What a banker can ethically tell you is what the loan value is on a particular boat. Most banks will only loan a maximum of wholesale cost on a boat and would prefer to loan a little less. The theory is that in the event of a default on a boat loan, the collateral can be disposed of without the bank having to price the used boat so high that it is an unattractive value compared to the same vessel new.

Commissioning Costs

When making an offer on a new boat, keep the cost of commissioning the boat in mind. Dock lines, fenders, life jackets, tool sets, spare parts, flares, first-aid kits, an anchor and rode will all need to be brought aboard before the maiden voyage commences, as well as a suitable dinghy. A new boat will usually be delivered without any canvas to cover the bridge, windows, and hatches and may be lacking interior curtains or blinds as well. Commissioning costs can easily add at least a few thousand dollars to a new boat, and substantially more when a new dinghy and outboard motor are factored in.

Emotional Control

When making an offer on a new boat there is an aspect of negotiation to bear in mind. It is no more likely that the yacht brokerage or seller will accept the first low-ball offer than it is likely the buyer will have to pay full sticker price for a boat. Making an outrageously low offer is an excellent way to begin the price negotiation, but many buyers fall into the psychological trap of becoming emotionally involved with their offer once it has been presented. The buyer suddenly considers every dollar spent above what began as a calculated, deliberately unrealistic bargaining ploy as a personally defeating slap to the ego. Maintain your

Commissioning costs can easily add a couple of thousand dollars to a new boat.

cool. The negotiating advantage usually accrues to the party with the most emotional control. The purchase of the boat is ordinarily just the first of many transactions which can take place with the local brokerage for a particular manufacturer. Make a deal without making any enemies.

USED-BOAT VALUES

Determining a value on a used boat is more complex. While the year of production may be of some minor interest in the equation, and the manufacturer is certainly important, no two 10-year-old Northern Explorer sportfishermen will ever be worth exactly the same. Overall condition will vary widely from one vessel to another, as will engine hours and optional equipment. It can be useful to compare pricing on a large number of similar-sized and general-type boats and thus develop a feel for the going prices in a certain category. Some boats are popular enough and so widely available on the used market that it is practical to get a brand-specific education on used boat values. But knowing that "15-year-old 40-foot trawlers are typically advertised for between $80,000 and $120,000 in my local market" may establish an adequate range with which to establish a relative value. Pay little attention to anecdotal evidence such as "my next door neighbor works with a guy whose brother-in-law just bought a 3-year-old, 36-foot Goldenray for $35,000." It is remarkable just how predictably conversations regarding the fantastic deal just made (due to the low price paid or the high price collected) will allow the deal to become even more fantastic with each retelling.

Used-Boat Prices and Replacement Cost

A very broad market generalization finds most 5-year-old used boats selling for 60 percent of their current replacement prices, 10-year-old boats bringing about 40 percent, and 20-year-old boats commanding about 25 percent of current replacement costs. The three factors which affect this equation most prominently are condition, condition, and condition!

Effects of Time on Used-Boat Prices

Prices of used boats tend to decrease as a boat remains unsold. The seller's boundless optimism in the early weeks of the sales process may give way to a more realistic attitude as an initially overpriced boat garners no offers. Sellers who have already purchased another boat and who are possibly making two marine mortgage payments, paying two moorage fees, and insuring two boats may become particularly flexible as time advances. In climates where there is a particular boating season, an offer to purchase as the summer or fall cruising season is ending—and the present owner is facing the prospect of a winter's storage and/or financing costs—might buy a boat for a lower price than waiting until the buyer brigade begins walking the docks again in late winter and early spring.

Effect of Financed Balance on Price

Most used boats will have a marine mortgage that needs to be paid off when the new owner acquires the boat, and this is usually handled when the purchaser obtains new financing. The outstanding dollar balance of the loan on a vessel may affect the amount of room a particular seller feels he or she has in the price. Sellers who are only a few years into the payment schedule on a late-model boat with small down payments may owe so much that they will actually be unable to sell at or below fair market value. Many sellers are financially unable to take cash out of pocket at the time of sale to pay off the outstanding balance of the boat loan.

Using a Broker

Start low when determining an initial offering price on a used boat, but bear in mind that the seller has ego as well as money invested in the boat. A buyer who offers a price 40–50 percent under market value may so offend the seller that negotiations break down entirely. When making a very low offer on a used boat, the services of a yacht broker can be very valuable. The broker becomes the third party and can function as an emotionally uninvolved mediator to keep negotiations flowing smoothly.

TERMS FOR ANY OFFER

As previously noted, conditions which should be written into the offer include making the vessel available for sea trial, having the boat surveyed, arranging financing, and establishing a time line by which the buyer and seller must each complete their respective obligations. Be certain that adequate time is allowed for this. An offer should contain language specifying under what circumstances the buyer may call the transaction off and receive a refund of the initial deposit. From the buyer's perspective, the more broadly the terms are stated, the better. Some offers have even been written that allow the "purchaser to withdraw this offer at any time, for any cause or for no cause, up until the moment of closing and receive a full refund of purchaser's deposit." (A buyer might well question why a seller would agree to take a boat off the market without a firm commitment from the prospective purchaser.) Typically, an unsatisfactory sea trial, incurable defects discovered during survey, or the inability of the buyer to secure acceptable financing are considered reasonable conditions under which a buyer may withdraw from a sale. Most sellers are willing to correct the minor irregularities which will almost inevitably be discovered by a survey, rather than lose the sale entirely.

Legal Advice

An offer to purchase a boat is an important legal document, and it can be prudent to enlist the services of your attorney to review the terms and conditions before finalizing the offer. This is especially true when dealing directly with a private seller on a used boat, as any local or federal laws which would constrain certain questionable practices by brokers will not apply in a transaction between private individuals.

28

The Sea Trial

O NCE THE CONDITIONAL OFFER has been accepted, the first contingency which must be dealt with is the sea trial.

NEW-BOAT SEA TRIALS

Many people who purchase smaller day cruisers do so without a sea trial. A prudent buyer should insist on the right to an on-the-water demonstration of the boat's capabilities before final money changes hands. A reasonable seller should be willing to accommodate such a request. When purchasing a brand-new boat, the sea trial may actually be conducted on an identical vessel, already commissioned. In such a case, it may be wise to specify in the original offer that the vessel actually delivered will perform in a manner consistent with the boat which was used for sea trial.

USED-BOAT SEA TRIALS

On a used boat the offer should contain a clause requiring the boat to pass a mechanical as well as a hull survey. Your surveyors may prefer to be aboard for the sea trial, as there are certain observations which can be made when underway that might not be possible at the dock.

WEATHER CONSIDERATIONS

The most informative sea trials are conducted in moderate winds on somewhat choppy seas. Since most sellers will postpone the sea trial if gale warnings are displayed, it is just as reasonable for the buyer to reschedule if the water is as calm as a millpond with little or no wind. Unless a boater plans to go out strictly in life-threatening situations or on the few days a year when the weather is perfect, a sea trial conducted under either extreme will yield very little of the information the buyer is interested in. Determine how the boat handles under the normal (and maybe slightly worse-than-normal) conditions to which the boat will typically be subjected. Getting a good "sea-trial day" is easier when buying a boat in the winter. If the boat under trial throws a large enough wake or if there are a number of other boats in the vicinity creating reasonably large wakes, the resulting wave action can be a sort of substitute for a decent 10- to 20-knot wind. Using wakes instead of waves to test handling characteristics requires a lot of radical helmsmanship, including a number of sharp port and starboard turns into the boat's own wake.

STARTING THE ENGINES

It is better if the engines are not already warmed up when you arrive for a sea trial. If an engine is difficult to start when cold, a seller can conceal this by letting the engine run for 10 or 15 minutes before the buyer arrives. The temperature gauges should read at the extreme cold end of their range when the starting switch is first engaged.

When the engines are started and idling at the dock, this is an excellent time to examine the exhaust. On twin-engine boats the amount and color of exhaust should be about the same from both exhaust ports, and the exhaust should not be overly black or blue in color. Black exhaust is usually the by-product of an engine running too rich; blue exhaust is usually associated with oil burning due to worn rings, valve guides, or both. Diesel engines will have a visible exhaust smoke for the first few minutes following a cold start. A reasonable amount of cooling water should splash out every several seconds from any engine exhaust port. And again, on twin-engine boats the amount should be fairly equal, or one engine may have a raw-water cooling pump in need of replacement.

GETTING UNDERWAY

Most sellers or brokers will insist on handling the boat when leaving the dock. The potential for damage to the boat or other craft nearby is too great to turn the controls over to a helmsman unfamiliar with a specific vessel. While observing the process of getting underway, note which direction the winds and currents are flowing and what effect this seems to have on the maneuverability of the boat. A question such as "does this boat seem to be more susceptible to wind or to current when docking?" might serve to open some conversation regarding close-quarters handling and docking characteristics.

DEFINING CRUISING SPEED

In open water, the buyer should be allowed to take control of the boat. One item to perform during the trial will be a cruising speed survey. An aspect many sellers misrepresent, either through plain ignorance or by intent, is the speed at which a boat will cruise. Cruising speed is not top speed but a speed at which the engines can propel a boat through the water for extended periods of time without overheating or undue mechanical stress. Many diesel engines cruise comfortably at about 75–80 percent of their maximum rpm. Gasoline engines may red line at around

5500 rpm, but for normal sustained operation, most will give longer and more reliable service at no more than 60-70 percent of that number. The optimum usage of available engine rpms will vary by application, and manufacturer recommendations should be noted for various vessel and propeller combinations. The seller or broker should be able to furnish the rpm at which a boat will cruise, and the reliability of the information can be verified by keeping an eye on the temperature gauge.

The Speed Trial

Speed-indicating instruments on boats are seldom extremely accurate. A speed run will establish the cruising speed capabilities of a boat as well as indicate the amount of variation between actual speed made good and the speed indicated on the speed log or speedometer. In many areas, there are measured-mile markers where boats are taken for speed tests, but any course of known exact distance which can be established on a chart will do as well. While up to cruising speed, the boat enters the measured course from either end and a careful notation of the number of minutes and seconds required to run the course is made. The boat is then operated at the same rpm back through the course in the other direction and timed as well. By averaging the two elapsed times, the effects of wind and currents will be nullified and a speed can be determined. The formula for computing speed is 60 divided by the number of minutes per nautical mile equals speed. A 6-knot cruising speed covers a nautical mile in 10 minutes, a 10-knot cruiser does a mile in 6 minutes, 15 knots takes 4 minutes, 20 knots takes 3 minutes, and so on. (Fractional minutes must be converted into decimal equivalents before making the calculation. Divide 60 by the number of seconds to determine the decimal equivalent of the seconds elapsed.)

Top Speed

Top speed can be extrapolated accurately enough from cruising speed. It wouldn't be wise or even necessary to ever operate a boat with a wide open throttle for more than a few seconds at a time except for a racing situation. If a boat is listed with a cruising speed of 12 and a top speed of 14 and easily makes 12 during the speed survey, the 14 is probably technically achievable as well. A boat listed with a cruising speed of 8 and top speed of 10 that struggles to do a strong 7 during speed trial may have been misrepresented, may have had a prop change, or developed a fouled bottom since the last speed survey (possibly both), and probably won't do the 10 knots, either.

CIRCULAR SEA TRIALS

A recommended course in a sea trial is a large circle, perhaps a mile or so in diameter. Running this course once to starboard and once to port will expose a boat to head seas, quartering and beam seas both starboard and port, and following seas. Note how much the boat pitches or slams in head seas, rolls in beam or quartering seas, or tends to wallow and wander in following seas. Particularly on boats with hulls that have a tendency to plane, it is important to vary the speed of the vessel widely enough to experience the changes in handling characteristics. At the helm, the prospective buyer should feel comfortable with the visibility afforded for maneuvering in tight quarters.

MISCELLANEOUS TESTING

A sea trial provides an opportunity to check various systems aboard a boat which could not be adequately tested dockside. Autopilots and plotters can be tested while underway, and radar safely activated without concern for endangering people standing on a nearby dock.

LOAD FACTORS

During a sea trial it is important to note the amount of fuel and water aboard. A boat which appeals to a purchaser because "it cruises at 20 knots" should be able to do so with fuel and water tanks topped off, since no reasonable boater goes cruising with a nearly empty water tank and one-eighth of a tank of fuel. Sellers may be understandably reluctant to completely fuel a boat for sea trial, but filling the water tanks costs virtually nothing. If the boat with a large fuel capacity is low on fuel (and therefore lighter), you should expect that the advertised cruising speed will be reached very easily indeed. Optional equipment, a large group of people aboard, and a half-ton of pots, pans, canned goods, clothing, tools, and sporting goods stowed away will affect final performance as well.

CONCLUDING THE SEA TRIAL

The seller or broker will want to take the helm again when approaching the dock. Assuming that the boat has handled in a satisfactory manner, the performance has been as advertised and expected, and no major defects which the seller cannot or will not cure have been discovered, the buying process has evolved to the survey stage.

29

The Survey

THE SURVEY PROCESS BEGINS with hiring a surveyor. On a used vessel, it is prudent to use two surveyors: one for a hull survey and one for a mechanical survey. Very few surveyors will have the required knowledge to competently perform both surveys.

HULL SURVEY

Hull surveyors are charged with rendering an informed opinion, following a thorough inspection, of the structural soundness, overall condition, and, on a used vessel, an approximate value. A surveyor will list exceptions or defects discovered, and a buyer must be willing to accept that on anything as complex as a powerboat there will always be an opportunity to improve, repair, or replace some aspects or items. The items discovered in a survey may be as minor as "latch on transom door should be reattached with larger screws," or as major as "extensive laminate blistering throughout hull." It is the seller's responsibility to cure any defects discovered, and the buyer's prerogative to withdraw from the sale if the defects are major in nature and/or the seller is unwilling to make the required corrections. In some cases, defects discovered during survey are cured by the buyer, following an additional price concession by the seller. Most financial institutions and insurance companies will want to examine the survey report and be assured that any significant exceptions have been fixed before a loan is finalized or an insurance policy issued for a boat.

Hiring a Surveyor

To get a thorough and excellent hull survey, you must hire a thorough and excellent surveyor. If the broker says, "We always use Hoboken Smith to survey the boats we sell," be aware that Hoboken may feel greater loyalty to the broker's interests in the sale than to the buyer's. It might very well be that Mr. Smith is the most qualified surveyor available, and if so there would be no particular reason to avoid using his services. However, it is a sad fact that in many localities a man can be a butcher or a cab driver on Saturday, print some business cards and hang up a sign on Sunday, and be a marine surveyor on Monday. Some of these "surveyors" are back driving cab, cutting meat, or have taken up real estate appraisal 30 days later. So it can be important when hiring a surveyor to ask for some references and to inquire as to the length of applicable professional experience.

Certified Surveyors

Many of the more reputable and capable surveyors belong to one or more of the national organizations which certify surveyors, such as the National Association of Marine Surveyors, the Society of American Marine Surveyors, or the American Boat and Yacht Council.

Locating a Surveyor

Marine insurance companies routinely require boats that they have insured for several years to be periodically re-surveyed to detect deteriorating conditions which might ultimately result in large insurance losses. Most marine insurance companies can recommend particular surveyors with whom they have had good experience. Unless you live in a very small community, it may be necessary to get four or five recommendations on surveyors before an individual name begins to stand out. Some surveyors in a given area may be specialists or particular experts in a field such as wooden hulls, and could be the best choice depending on individual circumstances.

Hauling Out

To perform a thorough survey, the surveyor will need access to the bottom of the boat and it will be necessary to have the vessel hauled, an expense commonly absorbed by the buyer. The surveyor will spend considerable time tapping the hull with a small mallet in order to listen for any changes in sound which might indicate a decaying wooden member or a section of delaminating fiberglass. For most boaters, there are few opportunities to examine the underside of their boats without donning fins and snorkel, and the survey haul-out is a great opportunity to become familiar with a vessel below the waterline.

MECHANICAL SURVEY

An engine and marine-transmission survey can be conducted by an expert mechanic familiar with the particular brand of engine aboard. Major engine manufacturers will usually have a dealer for their particular product in an area, and this dealer will ordinarily have the most informed personnel available to analyze the condition of their franchised brand of engine. Ask for a cost estimate for any recommended adjustments or repairs, as these are items which can properly be topics for negotiation with the broker or seller. The engine surveyor will typically want to withdraw a couple of ounces of crankcase oil to be sent to a laboratory for analysis. A good oil analysis, properly interpreted, will be extremely useful in arriving at a well-founded opinion of an engine's mechanical condition. When the engine surveyor is aboard, don't forget to have the generator inspected as well.

30

Wrapping Up the Deal

W ITH AN ACCEPTABLE SURVEY in hand, or the survey of a used boat where the seller has corrected any noted exceptions, the paperwork process begins. The required forms and documents will typically be prepared either by a marine mortgage company or the lending officer of a local bank.

THE MARINE MORTGAGE

For the majority of boaters, much of the paperwork revolves around the processing of a boat loan or marine mortgage. The lender will almost always require a copy of the surveyor's report and valuation when financing a used boat. A knowledgeable lender will want some evidence that the work called for in the survey has been completed and will require some proof of insurance coverage as well.

INSURANCE

Shop for insurance. Various underwriting companies evaluate risks differently and insurance premiums are not even close to standardized for any class of boat throughout the industry. While marine insurance brokers would have you believe that "everybody's rates are about the same; the difference is service and ours is the best," first-hand experience indicates that some insurance quotes can be as much as double those of other companies. Marine insurance policies usually carry at least a 1 percent deductible, ($1,500 on a $150,000 boat), so while marine repairs are expensive, a boater will not be involving the insurance company in every little scratch or scrape that results from bumping the dock during a difficult landing. Boaters in areas where hurricanes occur with any frequency will pay more for marine insurance than boaters who restrict their cruising to relatively calm, inland waters with less hazardous weather patterns.

DOCUMENTATION

Boats will either be documented by the Coast Guard or titled and registered with the state government in which the boat is permanently moored. Coast Guard documentation is a way of registering a vessel in a country (the U.S.) rather than registering the vessel in a particular state. In states where an annual excise tax is collected on boats, even vessels which are Coast Guard documented and have never been issued a state title are usually required to obtain a certificate of state registration and pay the annual tax.

SALES TAX

A majority of states collect a sales tax when a boat is sold. A few boaters cook up elaborate schemes to register their boats in states where there is no sales tax, but this approach is seldom practical or ultimately successful. Sales-tax states have fairly universally adopted laws which require either sales tax or an equivalent use tax to be paid on a boat that remains in state waters for more than 60 or 90 days, unless it can be established that sales tax has already been paid elsewhere. Boaters who relocate to a state with higher sales taxes may discover that they must pay a tax equal to the difference in the sales tax paid in the state of purchase and the sales tax due in the state of new residence. Unfortunately, boaters moving from a high sales-tax state into a lower sales-tax state cannot expect a corresponding refund!

CHARTER BOAT TAX BREAKS

In many states there is no sales tax on boats purchased for commercial operation or for use as charter. To prevent the complete loss of tax revenue that would result from every boater declaring a new vessel is being purchased "for charter," a state will ordinarily require a business license be obtained and will collect sales taxes on both the revenues developed from the chartering operations and a use tax due when the owner of a commercial charter vessel uses the boat for personal rather than business purposes. Insurance premiums and finance interest rates will both be higher for commercial boats, so going commercial is a poor tax dodge indeed.

LEGAL ADVICE

Dealing with the majority of banks and major finance institutions is usually a low-risk proposition, but for those boaters who feel more comfortable discussing the forms and documents with an attorney, this is the opportunity to do so. Most large institutions will resist rewriting a loan document to change verbiage or clauses which a buyer's attorney doesn't like (they would, after all, have to run any changes past their own attorneys), but at least the legally counseled borrower can be prepared to sign the loan agreement with a full understanding of the terms and conditions it contains.

31

Congratulations

You're a boater! You and your family are in for some adventures that will create lifetime memories. May they all be pleasant memories.

TAKING DELIVERY

In most boating communities it is possible to take some on-the-water training in basic boat handling from certified instructors. During the time between the offer to purchase being accepted and the day of delivery, some training for a novice skipper is well advised. Unless you are quite justifiably confident of your ability to handle your new boat, it is a good idea to enlist a qualified friend or even hire a licensed captain to assist when taking delivery. Your fellow boaters will have little or no patience for any damage done when a beginner careens down the fairway learning to navigate by the Braille method. Before leaving the dock, make certain that all required Coast Guard equipment is aboard, including a life jacket for everybody, and be cognizant of the locations of fire extinguishers and the first-aid kit. Most brokers will assist in helping a new boater become familiar with the controls and instrumentation of a newly acquired vessel.

SHAKEDOWN CRUISES

It could be a mistake to pick up a freshly acquired boat on the first day of a summer's vacation and set out on a lengthy cruise to a remote anchorage. A few local shakedown journeys would be better, allowing a boater to become familiar with the vessel's operational tendencies and to put all of the systems through an initial, real-world test.

YACHT CLUBS

Consider joining a yacht club. Most yacht clubs don't fit the stereotypical image of a group of business tycoons sitting around in blue blazers and white slacks, polishing their brass buttons and looking down their disapproving noses at the rest of mankind. In most clubs, a fairly congenial atmosphere prevails among a group of genuinely nice people (boating tends to be a fairly humbling experience), and the majority of members really perceive themselves as "boaters" rather than "yachtsmen." A new boater could do far worse than to develop a couple of dozen more experienced friends willing to share their knowledge and experiences and shorten the learning curve considerably. While some clubs can be prohibitively expensive or require a fairly blue-blooded personal pedigree, the majority of yacht clubs are not ridiculously exclusive or beyond the financial means of most boaters.

See you on the water...

Index

fuel lines, 86
fuel systems, 81–86
fuel tanks, 81–82

galleys, 10, 131–34
gas engines: carbureted vs. fuel-injected, 42; characteristics of, 41–42; cold-starting of, 164–65; cruising speed and, 165–66; engine hours on, 42; hazards of, 42; longevity of, 41. *See also* diesel engines generators. *See* electrical systems, generators in
GPS, 143–44

heat exchangers, 87, 88
heaters: diesel furnaces, 112; electric, 111; free-standing fireplaces, 112; hot-water radiators, 111; propane heaters, 112
heating (and cooling), 7, 109–15; calculation of BTU's for, 110; regional considerations for, 109–10
helm stations, inside vs. fly bridge, 7
holding tanks. See sanitation systems, holding tanks in
hull designs, 27–32. *See also* planing hulls; semi-displacement hulls; displacement hulls; hull speed; bow designs; stern and chine designs
hull materials, 8, 33–36. *See also* composites, plywood-fiberglass; fiberglass; wood
hull speed: computation of, 29; twin engines and, 39

instrumentation, engine, 135–40; alarms for, 135–136; analog vs. digital, 135; and engine-hour meters, 138–39; and fuel gauges, 136–37; and oil-tem-perature gauges, 139–40; and speedometers, 137–38; and temperature, oil-pressure, and tachometer gauges, 136; and voltmeters, 137
insurance, 173–74
intercoms, 146

length, water line vs. overall, 15
Loran, 138, 145

moorage, 11, 46
motoryachts, 19, 25–26

navigation, 141–46; charts and compasses for, 141; GPS and, 143–44

offers, 155–62; bank loan values and, 157–58; brokers and, 161; consideration of commissioning costs and, 158; elements of, 155; negotiations in, 158–59; for new boats, 156; terms for, 161–62; for used boats, 159–61

planing hulls, 17, 27–28; seaworthiness of, 28; speed and, 27
powerboats: depreciation/inflation and, 49; fuel costs for, 47; miscellaneous expenses of, 46–47; size of, 11–15; tax laws and, 45; varieties of, 17–26. *See also* boats; *and specific types*
prices, 156–62; at boat shows, 157; new boat, 156; used-boat, 159–61
primary systems, 60–115; definition of, 60; inspection of, 60–115. *See also specific systems*
propane, 132–34; lines, 134; lockers, 133; safety concerns and,